Received on

OCT 3 0 2016

Green Lake Library

NO LONGER PROPERTY OF
THE SEATTLE PUBLIC LIBRARY

D1006527

What the Dickens?!

WHAT
THE
DICKENS?!

DISTINCTLY DICKENSIAN WORDS
AND HOW TO USE THEM

by Bryan Kozlowski

RUNNING PRESS
PHILADELPHIA · LONDON

© 2016 by Bryan Kozlowski

Published by Running Press,
An Imprint of Perseus Books, a Division of PBG Publishing, LLC,
A Subsidiary of Hachette Book Group, Inc.

All rights reserved under the Pan-American and International Copyright Conventions

Printed in Canada

*This book may not be reproduced in whole or in part, in any form or by any means,
electronic or mechanical, including photocopying, recording, or by any information
storage and retrieval system now known or hereafter invented, without written
permission from the publisher.*

Books published by Running Press are available at special discounts for bulk
purchases in the United States by corporations, institutions, and other organizations.
For more information, please contact the Special Markets Department at the Perseus
Books Group, 2300 Chestnut Street, Suite 200, Philadelphia, PA 19103, or call
(800) 810-4145, ext. 5000, or e-mail special.markets@perseusbooks.com.

ISBN 978-0-7624-6077-9
Library of Congress Control Number: 2016944190

E-book ISBN 978-0-7624-6112-7

9   8   7   6   5   4   3   2   1
Digit on the right indicates the number of this printing

Designed by Jason Kayser
Edited by Zachary Leibman
Typography: Darnalis, Helsing, and Stemple Schneidler

Running Press Book Publishers
2300 Chestnut Street
Philadelphia, PA 19103-4371

Visit us on the web!
www.runningpress.com

What words can paint tremendous truths like these!

—Charles Dickens

Every language has its limits. Just ask Pip in *Great Expectations*. When Estella humiliates the heart out of him, he can't seem to find a word to fit his feelings. Is he "humiliated, hurt, spurned, offended, angry, sorry"? One simple word would surely help to make sense of it all. But try as he might, Pip cannot "hit upon the right name" to describe the pain, and tears start puddling in his eyes. It was a frustration that his creator, Charles Dickens, knew all too well.

For almost four decades, Dickens grappled with Pip's predicament on a daily basis: searching for the perfect words in a language that seemed far too small for life itself. And life was exactly what Dickens was striving to capture. From homely fireside gatherings to late-night strolls through London, Dickens only "dwelt upon . . . familiar things," knowing full well that familiar things are always the hardest to describe. That Dickens described them better than anyone else, however, is obvious through his extraordinary legacy. For most people, the Victorian world *is* Dickensian. And it took a tremendous amount of words to practically brand an entire century. An estimated four million words, in fact, shape the world of Dickens' novels, to say nothing of his equally enormous output of short stories, articles, plays, speeches, and personal letters. No wonder his autobiographical hero, David Copperfield, admits, "I wallow in words."

Dickens wallowed in words like no other. Academically unorthodox, he mastered English by manipulating it: stretching its conventions and rules of grammar whenever needed, and rifling through the world of slangs and colloquialisms when conventional English failed him. When slang itself failed to capture life, Dickens invented new words and phrases with such astonishing dexterity, it seemed as if they had always existed (with most, of course, going on to be embraced by conventional English itself). In short, to read and listen to Dickens stories in the nineteenth century was to experience some of the most cutting-edge language of the times. It was a language of familiar things, but it seemed entirely new.

Two centuries later, Dickens' language has come full circle. It is now old enough to be new again, to be as fresh and charming (and often as confusing) to the modern reader as it was for the average Victorian. Albeit slightly more confusing today, Dickens' words continue to do what all languages do best, becoming timeless snapshots of the culture, people, history, and customs of their world. And what these words reveal about Dickens' literary landscape—his foggy streets, his sooty London, his warmhearted heroes, and icy villains—are stories within stories themselves.

As such, it seems only fitting to approach Dickens' words as Dickens approached his world, not as a dictionary, but as a linguistic tour through the light and dark corners of the Dickensian experience:

through merriment and hardships, poverty and wealth, ignorance and understanding.

In the end, we can't promise to make you another Mr. Micawber with his "superfluous establishment of words," but we can promise not to wallow in them. Dickens got *that* out of the way for us and it is now our pleasure to simply delight in the quirky effusions of his remarkable pen. In essence, let us take our cue from the logophilic "literary ladies" in *Martin Chuzzlewit*, who "splashed up words in all directions, and floundered about famously."

"It Was the Best of Times"

WORDS FOR MAKING MERRY

Bonneting

[BON-uh-ting] Any cap-related jest, usually involving knocking a man's hat off, or pulling it down over his eyes, a favorite antic of Victorian troublemakers.

> *"What!" exclaimed the Ghost . . . "Is it not enough that you are one of those whose passions made this cap, and force me through whole trains of years to wear it low upon my brow!" Scrooge reverently disclaimed all intention to offend or any knowledge of having wilfully "bonneted" the Spirit at any period of his life.*
>
> **— A CHRISTMAS CAROL**

No wonder Scrooge is quick to disavow any act of bonneting. Not only did it squash a perfectly good hat, it also squashed whatever the man happened to be keeping up there. Hats, after all, were portable storage places for nineteenth-century men. Some were quite roomy for the purpose, with top hats reaching up to fourteen inches high in the early eighteen hundreds. Naturally, many Dickensian characters make good use of the space, keeping everything from hot rolls and ham to a whole junk drawer of "crumpled documents" in their caps. David Copperfield, however, has the most gallant idea of the bunch, namely, "buying a bouquet for Dora" and placing it "in my hat, to keep it fresh."

Bumper

[BUHM-per] A glass filled to the brim.

---

*Mr. Tupple requests that every gentleman will do him the favour of filling his glass, for he has a toast to propose . . . He begs them to drain a **bumper** to "The Ladies, and a happy new year to them!"*

— SKETCHES BY BOZ

Oh dear, Mr. Tupple would probably consider our definition of a *bumper* a bit too skimpy for the occasion. And he'd be right. According to the unwritten rules of Victorian drinking habits, a bumper wasn't a proper bumper until your glass was filled just slightly *above* the brim—not quite enough for a spillover but just enough to reach that delicate point where the surface of the liquid forms a convex "bump" at the top of the glass, hence the name. Stagg from *Barnaby Rudge* seems to have mastered the art: "filling out a bumper without spilling a drop, by reason that he held his little finger at the brim of the glass, and stopped at the instant the liquor touched it." Obviously, maneuvering such a precarious pour out to your lips would certainly demand the steadiest of hands and concentration, which is why bumpers also served a dual purpose as one of the most reliable (and cleverly respectable) sobriety tests of nineteenth-century dinner parties. Spill just a drop and you might be victim to the dreaded sideways whisper: "Poor Mr. So-and-So, he can't hold his bumpers!"

Eleemosynary

[el-uh-MOS-uh-ner-ee] Charitable, derived from the Greek *eleos*, "pity"—the eventual root of the English word "alms."

I have just embarked in a design . . . to smoothe the rugged way of young laboureres, both in literature and the fine arts, and to soften, but by no **eleemosynary** *means, the declining years of meritorious age.*

— SPEECH BY CHARLES DICKENS (1851)

For an intensely generous man, and one who wrote the simple maxim, "No one is useless in this world . . . who lightens the burden of it for any one else," Dickens had a complex, if sometimes cynical, view of charity. Good intentions could easily go wrong, and misguided do-gooders were never safe from his scathing pen. In *Bleak House*, Mrs. Jellyby prefers to engage in "telescopic philanthropy," keeping a safe, comfortable distance between herself and the poverty she seeks to alleviate. Several chapters later, the formidable Mrs. Pardiggle goes to the opposite extreme, stomping into the dirtiest slums with her "rapacious benevolence" and bullying the poor into accepting her religiously loaded charity, whether they want it or not. For Dickens, if charity ever failed to preserve the dignity of those it sought to help, then it was usually "of that gunpowderous sort . . . the difference between it and animosity was hard to determine."

Gas and Gaiters

[gas·and·GAY-ters] Perfectly satisfactory, a nonsense verbalism coined by the crazed "old gentleman" in *Nicholas Nickleby*.

> *"Aha!" cried the old gentleman, folding his hands, and squeezing them with great force against each other. "I see her now; I see her now! My love, my life, my bride, my peerless beauty. She is come at last – at last – and all is **gas and gaiters**!"*
>
> — **NICHOLAS NICKLEBY**

Dickens' words might seem charmingly old-fashioned to us today, but we shouldn't forget how innovative they were in the nineteenth century. "Gas and gaiters" is a perfect example of why this is. At first, Victorians wouldn't have had a clue what it meant, nor would they know that "all is gas and gaiters" would soon become a popular idiom for "all is well with the world." But this uncertainty was indeed part of the original, almost quizzical, charm of reading Dickens. He didn't explain everything that came out of his characters' mouths, and readers were invited to take an active part in unriddling their idiosyncrasies. As such, the old gentleman's use of "gas and gaiters" is clearly not to be taken literally (this, after all, is the lunatic who requests a bottle of lightning and a thunder sandwich for lunch). But as with all nonsensical thoughts, it has a strange touch of sense about it, and "all is gas and gaiters" soon entered the Victorian lexicon.

Gormed

[gorhmd] Mr. Peggotty's private curse word in *David Copperfield*. Its literal translation would be "stupefied, confounded," from the English dialect verb *gorm*, "to stare blankly."

> *[Mr. Peggotty] swore a dreadful oath that he would be "**Gormed**" if . . . [his generosity] was ever mentioned again. It appeared, in answer to my inquiries, that nobody had the least idea of the etymology of this terrible verb passive to be gormed; but that they all regarded it as constituting a most solemn imprecation.*
>
> — DAVID COPPERFIELD

If you're looking for profanity in Dickens' fiction, you won't come any closer than "gormed." It's sort of like using "gosh-darned" today, as a substitute for the stronger expletive. Dickens knew that this sort of roughed-up vocabulary was all his sensitive Victorian readers could verbally stomach. And he promised, on more than one occasion, never to push those boundaries. "I endeavored," he wrote in the preface to *Oliver Twist*, "to banish from the lips of the lowest character I introduced, any expression that could by possibility offend." This is not to say that Dickens never had fun with his own censorship. You can almost hear him chuckling over this passage in *On Duty with Inspector Field*, where polite grammatical terms act as comic "bleeps" for one criminal's antipolice rant:

> *I won't, says Bark, have no adjective police and adjective strangers in my adjective premises! I won't, by adjective and substantive! Give me my trousers, and I'll send the whole adjective police to adjective and substantive!*

Gretna Green

[GRET-nuh·green] A small village in southern Scotland, straddling the English border, where marriage laws were far more lax, making it a favorite destination for eloping couples.

When Mr. Tappertit . . . saw [Dolly] come out of the house alone, such impulses came over him to decoy her into the chaise and drive off like mad, that he would unquestionably have done it, but for certain uneasy doubts besetting him as to the shortest way to **Gretna Green***.*

— BARNABY RUDGE

For late Georgian and early Victorian couples, running off to Gretna Green was a bit like passing through a drive-through wedding chapel in Las Vegas—marriages there were quick, cheap, and thrillingly daring. The daring part was escaping England's problematic marriage laws, where parents could veto their children's unions up until the young lovers reached the age of twenty-one. Once over the border in Scotland, however, those pesky English laws did not apply, and Gretna Green was waiting to greet all impatient lovebirds with open arms. There, boys could marry at fourteen and girls at twelve, with only two witnesses required to legally validate the marriage. Moreover, practically anyone could perform the hurried ceremony, even the local blacksmith. Indeed, having a blacksmith conduct the nuptials became somewhat of a Gretna Green tradition—the idea of him forging two hearts together, like two pieces of fiery metal, was irresistibly romantic to period sensibilities. This is why, of course, the cash-strapped Mr. Tappertit in *Barnaby Rudge* wonders whether "the blacksmith" in Gretna Green "would marry them on credit."

Gum-Tickler

[guhm·tik-ler] A strong, undiluted alcoholic drink, potent enough to "tickle" the gums in your mouth.

> *Mr. Venus, reminded of the duties of hospitality, produced some rum. In answer to the inquiry, "Will you mix it, Mr. Wegg?" that gentleman pleasantly rejoined, "I think not, sir. On so auspicious an occasion, I prefer to take it in the form of a **Gum-Tickler**."*
>
> — OUR MUTUAL FRIEND

Gum-Tickler took a while to materialize out of Dickens' vast vocabulary, as he likely heard it decades prior, while traveling through America in 1842. The word was first mentioned in an American travelogue,* along with other delightfully suggestive slangs for alcohol, such as "phlegm cutter," "gall-breaker," and "antifogmatic." The last deserves explanation. Antifogmatics originated in New England under the belief (or excuse) that a warming dose of liquor, first thing in the morning, would counteract the frigid effects of New England fogs. Dickens never got around to using the term, but he did record an equally charming expression he first heard in Boston—"Timber Doodle." While the actual drink was some ambiguous cocktail Dickens inevitably forgot the recipe for, the sound of Timber Doodle was obviously too cute to forget. In 1843, Timber Doodle became the name of Dickens' first and long-beloved dog.

---

*Travels Through Lower Canada, and the United States of North America by John Lambert, 1810

Harmonic Meeting

[hahr-MON-ik·MEE-ting] A jovial, rowdy gathering (of a musical nature, hence the "harmony") held in Victorian pubs.

---

*Mr. Micawber returned to the [prison] when his case was over, as some fees were to be settled, and some formalities observed, before he could be actually released. The club received him with transport, and held an **harmonic meeting** that evening in his honour.*

— DAVID COPPERFIELD

Pubs were at the epicenter of Victorian entertainment. Far more than neighborhood bars, they were, as their full name implies, public houses: local community centers that hosted dances, social clubs, literary discussions, and, of course, the odd "harmonic meeting." Also known as free-and-easies, harmonic meetings were incredibly popular in Dickens' time, though they really don't have a modern-day equivalent. The best we can do is to imagine them as something of an extended drinking song during which a roomful of men (this wasn't an occasion for respectable women) indulged in a night of bawdy, boisterous tunes and heavy drinking. Dickens describes "a hundred guests" at one "harmonic meeting" in *Sketches by Boz*, all "hammering" the tables with their beer mugs in rousing applause to the song just performed. They could very well have been singing one of Dickens' favorite harmonic selections, the all-popular "The Dog's Meat Man" song, which recounts the comic history of an old maid "with a face like tan" who "fell in love with the dog's-meat man."

Heeltap

[HEEL-tap] A small amount of liquor remaining at the bottom of a glass.

---

*"Beg your pardon, sir," said the stranger, "bottle stands—pass it round—way of the sun—through the button-hole—no **heeltaps**," and he emptied his glass, which he had filled about two minutes before, and poured out another, with the air of a man who was used to it.**

— THE PICKWICK PAPERS

The Victorians were a sensitive lot, especially when it came to their drinks. Leaving just a hint of a "heeltap" at the bottom of your glass was seen as a silent and unsociable indicator that you didn't like what your host was pouring out. Originally a cobbler's term, heeltaps were small pieces of leather fastened onto the bottom of shoes, and all subsequent ties between drinking and heeltaps were simply variations on "bottoms up!"—or heels up, for that matter. Of course, your mouth would start tasting like a well-worn piece of shoe leather if you carried out every "no heeltaps" command. But then again, you wouldn't be injuring any delicate Victorian feelings, and that was far more important.

---

*For Mr. Jingle's other drinking injunctions: "way of the sun" means clockwise, the proper way to pass a bottle around nineteenth-century tables. "Through the button-hole" is trickier. It likely meant "through the mouth," but could be another allusion to passing the bottle from right to left, as men's buttonholes are traditionally placed on the left side of their shirts.

Hippo-comedietta

[HIP-oh·kom-i-dee-ET-uh] A comic circus routine performed on horseback, from *hippo,* Greek for "horse," and *comedietta*, Italian for "small comedy."

> *The same Signor Jupe was to . . . wind them up by appearing in his favourite character of Mr. William Button . . . in "the highly novel and laughable **hippo-comedietta** of The Tailor's Journey to Brentford."*
>
> **— HARD TIMES**

Following the horseback-riding misadventures of Billy Button, a gangly tailor who can't seem to keep his hapless bum in the saddle, "The Tailor's Journey to Brentford" was *the* comedy act of Victorian circuses. A shamelessly recycled classic—sort of like the clown-car skit today—it simply never got old. And that's rather impressive, given that the "Tailor's Journey" was first performed in 1768—nearly a century before Signor Jupe still considered the act "highly novel." It made its creator, Philip Astley, famous and put Astley's Amphitheatre on the entertainment map as the most renowned equestrian circus in London, a spot it held for over one hundred years. Everything at Astley's "was delightful, splendid, and surprising!" wrote Dickens in *The Old Curiosity Shop*. Not a bad advertisement, and one that Astley's was quick to reciprocate. Soon, Dickensian characters from *Oliver Twist* and *The Pickwick Papers* were seen appearing in Astley's equestrian shows.

Hobbledehoy

[HOB-uhl-dee-hoi] An awkward and clumsy youth, of unknown origin, but possibly deriving from *hobidy-booby*, an archaic English dialect word for "scarecrow."

---

*All the Pickwickians were in most blooming array; and there was a terrific roaring on the grass in front of the house, occasioned by all the men, boys, and **hobbledehoys** attached to the farm.*

— THE PICKWICK PAPERS

Literature's best definition for a hobbledehoy comes from the pen of Dickens' friend and fellow writer Anthony Trollope in his 1864 novel, *The Small House at Allington*:

Such young men are often awkward, ungainly, and not yet formed in their gait; they straggle with their limbs, and are shy; words do not come to them with ease, when words are required, among any but their accustomed associates. Social meetings are periods of penance to them, and any appearance in public will unnerve them. They go much about alone, and blush when women speak to them. In truth, they are not as yet men, whatever the number may be of their years; and, as they are no longer boys, the world has found for them the ungraceful name of hobbledehoy.

Humbug

[HUHM-buhg] Nonsense, with the added Victorian meaning of a deceptive "hoax" or "fraud."

---

*"He said that Christmas was a **humbug**, as I live!" cried Scrooge's nephew. "He believed it too!"*

— A CHRISTMAS CAROL

Humbug might only come up a handful of times in *A Christmas Carol*, but the word has managed to become so nostalgically wrapped up with Dickens, with his all-surpassing character of Scrooge, even with Christmas itself, that Dickens seems to have invented the word and put a seasonal trademark on it forever. It's a lovely thought, but an incorrect one. The word *humbug* was almost one hundred years old by the time Dickens got his hands on it. He does, however, use it in an incredibly clever way, weaving its original connotations into the very plot of the story. As *humbug* likely derives from the English dialect words *hum*, "to deceive," and *bug*, "a ghost or goblin," Scrooge's insistence, at the start of the story, that Christmas is a "humbug," is literally akin to him saying that Christmas is a deceptive ghost. Nothing like tempting a few yuletide spirits, Ebenezer!

Joe Miller

[joh·MIL-er] A legendary jester. Joe Miller was a famous eighteenth-century actor, who was even more famous for his lack of humor. Because of this, upon his death, his name was ironically attached to a popular joke book, *Joe Miller's Jests*.

---

*"I'll send it to Bob Cratchit's!" whispered Scrooge, rubbing his hands, and splitting with a laugh. "He shan't know who sends it. It's twice the size of Tiny Tim. **Joe Miller** never made such a joke as sending it to Bob's will be!"*

— A CHRISTMAS CAROL

When it was first published in 1739, *Joe Miller's Jests* had society roaring with laughter. Its collection of more than two hundred jokes and witticisms was sharp, wonderfully coarse, and a bit bawdy—just the sort of material you'd want to recycle at the next party. The only problem was everyone else had the same idea. And by Dickens' day, the name "Joe Miller" was far more synonymous with old, tacky jokes, along the hackneyed lines of "why'd the chicken cross the road?" But you can decide for yourself. Here's one of the book's more famous quips:

A lady's age happening to be questioned, she affirmed, she was but forty, and called upon a gentleman that was in company, for his opinion: Cousin, said she, do you believe I am in the right when I say I am but forty? I am sure, madam, replied he, I ought not to dispute it; for I have constantly heard you say so for above these ten years.

Jorum

[JOHR-uhm] A large drinking bowl, likely based on "Joram," a minor biblical character in the second book of Samuel who brought Kind David "vessels of silver, and vessels of gold."

---

*At the same table, with both her elbows upon it, was Mrs. Jiniwin; no longer sipping other people's punch feloniously with teaspoons, but taking deep draughts from a **jorum** of her own.*

— THE OLD CURIOSITY SHOP

A lover of punch, with enthusiasm rivaling that of even Mrs. Jiniwin, Dickens shared his own recipe with a woman friend in 1847 in the cheeky hopes of making her "a beautiful Punchmaker in more senses than one": First you'll need "a very strong common basin"—one that you don't mind breaking "in case of accident." Toss in the peel of three lemons, "cut very thin," a pint of "good old rum," a wineglass of brandy, and two handfuls of lump sugar (noting that Dickens had rather small hands). Proceed to "Set this on fire," letting the concoction "burn for three or four minutes at least." Give the punch another five minutes' rest after you've squeezed in the juice of the three lemons and added a quart of boiling water. "At this crisis . . . you may taste," adding more "sugar to your liking." Heat the punch (covered) for fifteen minutes and serve it hot, "but not too hot." Dickens ends by seemingly assuaging the concerns of greedy Mrs. Jiniwin herself: "These proportions and directions will, of course, apply to any quantity."

Kickshaw

[KIK-shaw] Dainty, delicate, an anglicized rendering of the French *quelque chose*, "something," with its more English connotations of "a little something."

> *Mr. Sapsea has been received at the Gate House with kindred hospitality; and on that occasion Mr. Jasper seated himself at the piano, and sang to him . . . no **kickshaw** ditties, favourites with national enemies, but gave him the genuine George the Third.*
>
> **— THE MYSTERY OF EDWIN DROOD**

The "genuine George the Third" is obviously a patriotic song, as it makes battle-crying allusions to reducing "to a smashed condition all other islands but this island." The best real-life contenders for the song could be either "Rule, Britannia" or "Hearts of Oak," both of which were written in the lifetime of King George III (1738–1820) and remained incredibly popular in the Victorian era. The ambiguity lies in the fact that there were a staggering number of patriotic songs and popular ballads being circulated in the nineteenth century, and we can't say for certain which song Dickens was actually referencing. This uncertainty was a dilemma faced by many Victorians as well—though not one without an easy solution. Namely, "ballad sellers" were positioned on almost every street in London and, in exchange for a small fee, they would teach you any popular song of the day. In *Our Mutual Friend*, the same service is provided by Silas Wegg, whose vast repertoire of melodies is particularly admired by Mr. Boffin: "Why, you know every one of these songs by name and by tune, and if you want to read or to sing any one on 'em off straight, you've only to whip on your spectacles and do it!"

Laocoön

[lay-OK-oh-wohn] One who is hopelessly entangled.

---

*"I don't know what to do." cried Scrooge, laughing and crying in the same breath; and making a perfect **Laocoön** of himself with his stockings. "I am as light as a feather, I am as happy as an angel, I am as merry as a schoolboy. I am as giddy as a drunken man. A Merry Christmas to everybody. A Happy New Year to all the world."*

— A CHRISTMAS CAROL

Adding the word "Laocoön" here was an afterthought for Dickens—hardly surprising as Scrooge's happy ending wouldn't, at first, seem appropriate for one of the most tragic allusions in classic mythology. In Virgil's *Aeneid*, Laocoön was a high priest of Troy, ruthlessly punished for simply being right. Warning his fellow Trojans not to accept the infamous wooden horse, his cautionary proverb against "Greeks bearing gifts" is still with us today. For that timeless bit of forethought, Laocoön incurred the anger of the goddess Athena (divine patron of the attacking Greeks), who summoned a pair of sea serpents to quickly shut him up. By the entwining of these snakes around Laocoön and his two sons, the idea of death by encoilment became Laocoön's contribution to classic myth. Most Victorians would have known the image, captured in the ancient marble statue of Laocoön and His Sons (unearthed in Rome in 1506)—one of the era's most recognizable images of antiquity and certainly Dickens' visual inspiration for Scrooge's own Christmas-morning scramble with a pair of serpentine stockings.

Marplot

[MAHR-plot] A meddlesome, though well-meaning, person who unwittingly spoils the plans of others, based on the comically nosy character in Susanna Centlivre's eighteenth-century play, *The Busie Body*.

> *"We must make haste to get out, Margaretta, my dear, or we shall be descended on by Mrs. Sprodgkin." To which Mrs. Milvey replied, in her pleasantly emphatic way, "Oh YES, for she IS such a **marplot**, Frank, and DOES worry so!"*
>
> — OUR MUTUAL FRIEND

If not for the memorable character of Marplot, Centlivre's play would never have been so phenomenally successful (it was still popular in Dickens' day). Indeed, Dickens took a page out of that strategic playbook when setting out on his own literary career. His first novel, *The Pickwick Papers*, written in serial installments, started off as quite a flop. With a loosely structured plot of disjointed comic episodes, *The Pickwick Papers* desperately needed its own Marplot—an intensely original character who could pass from the page into every reader's heart. Dickens famously responded to this need by creating Sam Weller. Introduced in chapter ten, this funny, street-smart servant to Mr. Pickwick brought a thematic cohesiveness to the sprawling comedy and sales of the serial began to skyrocket thereafter. Readers couldn't get enough of Sam's witty observations on life, especially his clever proverbs of comparison, now universally known as *Wellerisms*: "That's what I call a self-evident proposition, as the dog's–meat man said, when the housemaid told him he warn't a gentleman."

Marrow-bones and Cleavers

[MAR-oh-bohns·and·KLEE-verz] Rough, hideous music. The cacophonous sound of large heavy knives (cleavers) striking hollowed-out bones was a common musical accompaniment to Victorian weddings.

They were ready for a dance in half a second . . . when a combination of prodigious sounds was heard outside, and a good-humoured comely woman of some fifty years of age, or thereabouts, came running in . . . closely followed by the **marrow-bones and cleavers**.

— THE CHIMES

Quiet weddings were almost impossible to pull off in the nineteenth century. This, after all, was the era of professional wedding crashing, and if you wanted connubial peace and quiet, you had to pay for it. Thanks to an ancient custom of serenading newly married couples with obnoxious, makeshift instruments, Victorian wedding crashers armed themselves with tradition and made the most of every wedding they could. Uninvited and often complete strangers, they could show up at any point during the celebrations, clanging bells, banging drums, and striking marrow-bones as loudly and obnoxiously as they could. More obnoxious still, they demanded a bribe, or "fee," to stop playing, though this was usually doled out in a spirit of humorous goodwill. Still, marrow-boning was serious business for these rough musicians. The ones ready to crash Edith Granger's wedding in *Dombey and Son* are surprisingly organized, entering into business negotiations with the bride's household and settling their "terms" before the nuptials even take place. One would imagine they had all the leverage in the deal.

Moor-eeffoc

[MOOR-ee-fok] The uncanniness of common things seen suddenly from a different perspective. Case in point: *Moor-eeffoc* is simply the backward spelling of "coffee-room."

---

*I only recollect that . . . in the door there was an oval glass-plate, with COFFEE-ROOM painted on it, addressed towards the street. If I ever find myself in a very different kind of coffee room now, but where there is such an inscription on glass, and read it backward on the wrong side **MOOR-EEFFOC** (as I often used to do then, in a dismal reverie), a shock goes through my blood.*

— FROM DICKENS' ABANDONED AUTOBIOGRAPHY

Moor-eeffoc is the most elusive and enigmatic word in the Dickensian lexicon. Dickens himself didn't know how to define it, though future writers have linked it to the very heart of his creative legacy. The word was of deep significance to fantasy writers J.R.R. Tolkien and G.K. Chesterton—with the latter's definition still considered to be the best:

That wild word, 'Moor Eeffoc', is the motto of all effective realism; it is the masterpiece of the good realistic principle—the principle that the most fantastic thing of all is often the precise fact. And that elvish kind of realism Dickens adopted everywhere. His world was alive with inanimate object. The date on the door danced over Mr. Grewgious's, the knocker grinned at Mr. Scrooge, the Roman on the ceiling pointed down at Mr. Tulkinghorn, the elderly armchair leered at Tom Smart—these are all moor eeffocish things. A man sees them because he does not look at them.

Mr. Punch

[MIS-ter·puhnch] The most famous puppet in Victorian Britain. He, along with his wife Judy and a host of other characters, made up the Punch and Judy Show—an early example of slapstick comedy.

Now, the carriages arrive at the Bride's residence, and the players on the bells begin to jingle, and the band strikes up, and **Mr. Punch**, *that model of connubial bliss, salutes his wife.*

— DOMBEY AND SON

Punch puppet shows, arriving in England from Italy in 1662, were so ubiquitous on the streets of Victorian London that Dickens totally forgot to describe them. But essentially, they were the nineteenth-century version of Saturday morning cartoons—they had their variations, but the general formula went something like this: Mr. Punch appears on the stage and exchanges some cheeky banter with the audience before his wife, Judy, and Baby make their appearance. The Baby becomes fussy; Punch gets annoyed and tosses Baby out of the window. Judy isn't having any of that and starts bashing her husband's brains. Punch fights back and throws Judy out of the window for good measure, proclaiming, "That's the way to do it!" This act of domestic violence enrages the wider puppet community who try, each in their turn, to bring Punch to justice. But despite fighting with a local policeman, hangman, crocodile, and even the devil, Punch always prevails, dispatching each of his combatants with his famously flippant remark: "That's the way to do it!"—which, by then, every child in the audience was screaming out as well.

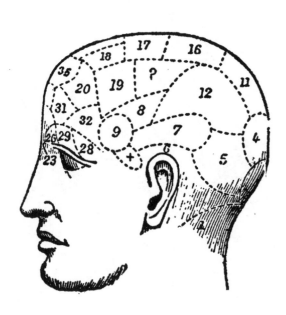

Organ of Benevolence

[OR-guhn·uhv·buh-NEV-uh-luhns] The head—more precisely, the area just above the forehead, that was believed to be the source of kindly and sympathetic feelings, according to the Victorian pseudoscience of phrenology.

---

*Old Fezziwig laid down his pen, and looked up at the clock, which pointed to the hour of seven. He rubbed his hands; adjusted his capacious waistcoat; [and] laughed all over himself, from his shoes to his **organ of benevolence**.*

— A CHRISTMAS CAROL

Phrenology, in Dickens' day, was an incredibly intriguing practice, acting as something of a cross between a psychic palm reading and a modern personality test. The logic ran thus: Since the brain was encapsulated in the skull, phrenologists believed every skull could be "read," with its unique shape offering clues to its owner's emotional and intellectual makeup. If different parts of the brain, known as "organs," were particularly active in certain individuals, an enlarged "bump" would correspondingly appear on the skull. Besides the organ of benevolence (which seems to have engulfed Mr. Fezziwig's entire head), there were the organs of *amativeness* ("sexual love"), of *philoprogenitiveness* ("parental love"), and of *vitativeness* ("love of life"), among numerous others. Of course, there were some bumps that even the best cranium reader couldn't figure out. In *Martin Chuzzlewit*, when Mr. Pecksniff takes a tumble down his front steps, his daughters rush to inspect his injuries. To their amazement, they find "the development of an entirely new organ, unknown to phrenologists, on the back of his head."

Over the Broomstick

[OH-ver·thuh·BROOM-stik] Married in a hasty, informal way.

---

*This woman [Molly] here had been married very young, **over the broomstick** (as we say), to a tramping man, and was a perfect fury in point of jealousy.*

— GREAT EXPECTATIONS

Everyone in Victorian England knew what Dickens was getting at with his "broomstick" reference. The wink, wink, nudge, nudge is that Molly was pregnant, hence the couple's need for a rushed wedding (too scandalous a thing to say outright in a nineteenth-century novel). Why Victorians associated broomsticks with scandal might seem odd for modern readers, given the fact that literally jumping over a broomstick is now a commonplace wedding tradition, especially in the African American community. But then again, we aren't as superstitious as Victorians were. Broomsticks, for them, were still hazily associated with pagan magic—a magic that linked broomsticks with fertility (thanks, in large part, to the obvious phallicism of the broom handle). As such, girls were superstitiously warned never to step over broomsticks, as the act could mysteriously make them pregnant. Whether this was a legitimate belief, or along the same lines as telling children that babies come from storks, is unclear, but the idea of brooms bringing unexpected babies stuck and "broomstick marriages" became the "shotgun weddings" of their day.

Porter and Skittles

[POHR-ter·and·SKIT-ulz] Fun and games, more literally "drink and games" with *porter* being a type of strong English beer and *skittles* a Victorian version of bowling. The expression, however, is more often rendered "beer and skittles" today.

> *"You see how these fellows drink, and smoke, and roar,"* replied Mr. Pickwick. *"It's quite impossible that they can mind it [prison] much."* *"Ah, that's just the wery thing, sir,"* rejoined Sam, *"they don't mind it; it's a reg'lar holiday to them—all* **porter and skittles.***"*
>
> **— THE PICKWICK PAPERS**

Those in search of some Dickensian fun and games should consult *A Christmas Carol*, a virtual textbook on how Victorians let their hair down. First, Bob Cratchit rushes home "to play at blindman's-buff," a boisterous game of tag in which the catcher is blindfolded while being mercilessly teased and pushed by other players (the old term *buff* signifying "a push or blow"). Then "there were forfeits" at Fezziwig's ball, forfeits being not so much a game as the penalty of losing a game. Players could forfeit money, though kisses were usually demanded instead (note how many hormonally hyper young people there are at Fezziwig's ball). Lastly, a few less-physical games are played at the house party of Scrooge's nephew. These are mostly memory and guessing games like "Yes and No" (a sort of twenty questions) and the closely related "How, When, and Where." These, too, are "Games of Forfeits" with kisses being the penalty (or reward) for the loser, especially for Mr. Topper, "a bachelor," who purposefully forfeits every game just to go after "that plump sister in the lace tucker."

Purl

[purl] A hot drink of sweetened beer flavored with gin and spices. Etymologically, it means a drink with bubbles on its surface, since purl is derived from the German *perlen*, "to bubble."

> *[The bar was] provided with comfortable fireside tin utensils, like models of sugar-loaf hats, made in that shape that they might, with their pointed ends, seek out for themselves glowing nooks in the depths of the red coals, when they mulled your ale, or heated for you those delectable drinks,* **Purl***, Flip, and Dog's Nose.*
>
> — OUR MUTUAL FRIEND

It's hard to imagine Dickens' fiction without the warm "delectable drinks" that sit steaming on the sideboards of his stories. But since Dickens rarely describes what goes into them, it's also hard to imagine how they would taste. So let's begin with the basics. "Flip" was essentially a warmed, spiked version of eggnog, without the cream. For "Dog's Nose," think of Purl (see definition) but leave out the sugar and spice. As for Dickens' frequent references to "negus"? That's a hot, lemon-and-nutmeg-infused punch with a base of sherry or port. Negus is served at the Fezziwig ball in *A Christmas Carol*, although Scrooge prefers a "bowl of Smoking Bishop"—a steamy compound of sweetened red wine and port flavored with clove-studded oranges. Some might consider Smoking Bishop a type of wassail today, though far different from the "mighty bowl of wassail" served at the Christmas party in *The Pickwick Papers* with its roasted "hot apples" bobbing in a "hissing and bubbling" brew of spiced ale—the sort of drink that makes Mr. Pickwick famously declare: "this is, indeed, comfort."

Rubber

[RUHB-er] In historic card games, a "rubber" is a set of three games, wherein winning two of the three games wins the entire set.

"Come, come," said the bustling host, with a natural anxiety to change the conversation,
*—"What say you to a **rubber**, Mr. Pickwick?"*

– THE PICKWICK PAPERS

So begins Mr. Pickwick's game of whist—that most "solemn observance" of Victorian card tables where players were prohibited from making unnecessary comments (*whist* is linguistically linked to an archaic English word for "silence"). Unsurprisingly, whist was rather boring to Dickens, it being too full of "gravity" to deserve "the title of 'game'" in his opinion. So he was quick to offer substitutes in other novels. In *Little Dorrit*, the lower classes entertain themselves with a rousing game of "all-fours"—one of the game's four scoring principles being the capture of the knave of trumps, called "Jacks" in this case. This is the game that likely taught Pip in *Great Expectations* the unfortunate habit of referring to all knaves as "Jacks"—a period faux pas that Estella is quick to chide him for during their own game of "beggar my neighbour," the aim of which was to rob one's opponent of all his cards. "Beggar him," cries Miss Havisham, never missing an opportunity to instruct her ward on the fine art of beggaring the male sex.

Sandboy

[SAND-boi] A proverbially happy person. Sandboys (Victorian sellers of sand for scouring and cleaning purposes) had a reputation for getting habitually drunk and, therefore, becoming habitually jolly afterwards.

---

*The Jolly Sandboys was a small road-side inn of pretty ancient date, with a sign, representing three **Sandboys** increasing their jollity with as many jugs of ale and bags of gold, creaking and swinging on its post on the opposite side of the road.*

— THE OLD CURIOSITY SHOP

No one can think of England's old roadside inns without thinking of Dickens. He made them famous, and few of his readers can't help but feel nostalgic for these "snugly-sheltered" havens that constantly "beckoned, Come in!" Nothing like a modern hotel, the Dickensian inn was a venerable home-away-from-home, one that cozily "tempted" the wary traveler "with many mute but significant assurances of a comfortable welcome." They appear, always just in time, in Dickens' colder passages, with a ruddy-faced innkeeper at the door offering hot food, warm drinks, and "Good beds." *The Pickwick Papers* is packed with such homely retreats, though the best old inn of Dickens' imagination has to be the Six Jolly Fellowship-Porters in *Our Mutual Friend*:

[It was] a very little room like a three-cornered hat, into which no direct ray of sun, moon, or star, ever penetrated, but which was superstitiously regarded as a sanctuary replete with comfort and retirement by gaslight, and on the door of which was therefore painted its alluring name: Cosy.

Sassigassity

[sas-eh-GAS-eh-tee] Audacity with attitude. A delightful Dickensian invention, blending the likes of "sassy," or "saucy," with "sagacious."

---

*Anon, the magic bell commands the music to cease, and the great green curtain rolls itself up majestically, and The Play begins! The devoted dog of Montargis avenges the death of his master . . . and a humorous Peasant with a red nose and a very little hat . . . remarks that the **sassigassity** of that dog is indeed surprising.*

— A CHRISTMAS TREE

Linguistically speaking, "sassigassity" is a hapax legomenon—a word used only once by an author, or occurring only once in a language. Dickens satisfied both criterions with "sassigassity," inventing it out of thin air for one short story and never using it again (more's the pity). But because he did this so frequently, Dickens' witty and limber manipulation of the English language seems almost routine. Many of his word inventions are rather useful, such as *metropolitaneously*, "in a city-like manner," and, of course, *adverbiously*, "overly verbose in the use of adverbs." Others are downright impossible to decipher; heaven knows what Dickens meant by "patientissamentally" in *Little Dorrit*. But most are simply there just to elicit a good laugh out of readers, much as they did for Dickens. After he had penned "sassigassity" to the page, he couldn't help but beam with the pride of a true inventor: "evermore this jocular conceit will live in my remembrance fresh and unfading, overtopping all possible jokes, unto the end of time."

Sir Roger de Coverley

[sur·Roj-er·duh·KUHV-er-lee] The most popular Christmas dance of the nineteenth century, though first appearing in the late 1600s.

> *But the great effect of the evening came after the Roast and Boiled, when the fiddler (an artful dog, mind! The sort of man who knew his business better than you or I could have told it him!) struck up "**Sir Roger de Coverley**."*

> — A CHRISTMAS CAROL

You can almost hear a good-humored groan resounding throughout the Fezziwig ball. Sir Roger de Coverley was to Victorian Christmas parties what the chicken dance is to modern wedding receptions. It was cheesy, predictable, and terribly overdone, though somehow it never failed to rouse a substantial group of giggling volunteers. First, they'd stand in two lines: ladies on one side, gents on the other, with those at the far ends designated as the "bottom" and "top" couple. Mr. and Mrs. Fezziwig, as presiding "top couple," stand at one end of a long line of twenty-four couples. They have "a good stiff piece of work cut out for them," says Dickens. And so they do, as most of the dance is solely performed by the top and bottom couple, who take five repeated turns meeting in the middle of the floor, while everyone else looks on. The top couple then weaves through the lines of dancers before a new top couple takes their place, beginning the dance all over again (and again and again, until every couple gets their chance to be on top). The dance at Fezziwig's would take nearly an hour to complete, hence all the groans at the start.

Snapdragon

[SNAP-drag-uhn] A Victorian parlor game, usually played at Christmas, wherein raisins are ignited in a shallow bowl of brandy to be quickly picked out and eaten without getting "snapped" (burned) by the swirling fire (the dragon).

---

*When they all tired of blind-man's buff, there was a great game at **snapdragon**, and when fingers enough were burned with that, and all the raisins were gone, they sat down by the huge fire of blazing logs to a substantial supper, and a mighty bowl of wassail.*

— THE PICKWICK PAPERS

The supposed "fun" of popping a flaming raisin into your mouth was certainly popularized by the Victorians (because, why not?—it *is* Christmas), but they didn't invent the lurid pastime. Nobody knows who did, though it certainly predates Dickens by some two hundred years: Shakespeare made two snapdragon references, calling it "flap-dragon"—another common name for the game. But no matter the century, playing snapdragon always came with its traditional hazards, usually "fingers . . . burned," though the risk, of course, was always much greater. In 1893, a game of snapdragon at a hospital in Surrey went horribly wrong, severely burning several people and killing a ten-year-old boy. Though the incident in Surrey took place after Dickens' time, snapdragon accidents like this must have made him extremely cautious. Dickens would never, after *The Pickwick Papers*, extoll the conflagrated joys of snapdragon again.

Snuggery

[SNUHG-uh-ree] A snug, comfortable place.

---

*If you don't mind paying for a bed . . . they'll make you up one on the **Snuggery** table, under the circumstances. If you'll come along, I'll introduce you there.*

— LITTLE DORRIT

A well-known and cherished part of Dickens' writing is the idea of "coziness" that pervades his every novel, casting a figurative "glow upon the faces gathered round the hearth" and drawing "each fireside group into a closer and more social league, against the roaring elements without" (*Battle of Life*). What's less known is how truly pervasive this idea was throughout Victorian society. To borrow a national slogan, privacy, of the snug and homely type, was the American Dream of the Victorian Englishman. "It is the Englishman who wishes to be by himself in his staircase as in his room," observed a French visitor to England in 1872, "[he] could not endure the promiscuous existence of our huge Parisian cages, and who, even in London, plans his house as a small castle, independent and enclosed."*

---

*Dickens would embody that ideal in *Great Expectations* with Mr. Wemmick's "castle," a tiny cottage in a London suburb built on "the idea of fortifications," boasting a miniature drawbridge and a ready supply of bacon around back, just in case the "little place" is "besieged."

Spanker

[SPANG-ker] Something very fine.

> *Mr. Sownds, the Beadle . . . asks if Mrs. Miff has heard it said, that the lady is uncommon handsome? The information Mrs. Miff has received, being of this nature, Mr. Sownds the Beadle, who, though orthodox and corpulent, is still an admirer of female beauty, observes, with unction, yes, he hears she is a* **spanker**—*an expression that seems somewhat forcible to Mrs. Miff.*
>
> — DOMBEY AND SON

Whatever Mrs. Miff thinks, Dickens highly enjoyed the word "spanker," also using the term in *Our Mutual Friend* and *Martin Chuzzlewit*. Its history predates these books by nearly two centuries, with *spanker* originally being a slang term for a gold coin—hence the word's gradual evolution to mean anything particularly fine or showy. But Mrs. Miff is probably right: applying the term to a lady would have been rather ungentlemanly for the times. This was mostly due to its bawdy subtext, acquired thanks to being tainted by association with Lady Gay Spanker, the leading female character in the famous 1841 play *London Assurance*. Domineering and uncomfortably sexual for the era, Lady Gay Spanker scandalized Victorian theatergoers who certainly weren't ignorant to the fact that "gay" was also a period euphemism for a woman of decidedly loose morals.

Spoony

[SPOO-nee] Lovesick in a silly or shallow way, in likely reference to the shallowness of a spoon.

> *Am I in love again? I am. I worship the eldest Miss Larkins. . . .*
> *My passion takes away my appetite . . . I even walk, on two or*
> *three occasions, in a sickly, **spoony** manner, round and round*
> *the house after the family are gone to bed, wondering which is*
> *the eldest Miss Larkins's chamber.*
>
> — DAVID COPPERFIELD

As Dickens most autobiographical character, David Copperfield and his spoony infatuations throughout the book were likely based on Dickens' real-life crush on Maria Beadnell. The pretty daughter of an affluent bank manager in London, Maria met Charles (then eighteen years old and a poor journalist) and instantly became the object of his self-proclaimed "fancy, romance, energy, passion" for three years. Though it proved to be a one-sided and eventually fruitless affair, Dickens wrote to Maria two decades later, candidly marking her out as one of the most propellant forces in his subsequent rise to fame: "It is a matter of perfect certainty to me that I began to fight my way out of poverty and obscurity, with one perpetual idea of you."

Stirrup-cup

[STUR-uhp-kuhp] A farewell drink, originally offered to guests before they set out on a journey (on horseback), after they had mounted the saddle and their feet were already in the stirrups.

Come, Mr. Neville, we are to drink to my nephew, Ned. As it is his foot that is in the stirrup—metaphorically—our **stirrup-cup** *is to be devoted to him."*

— THE MYSTERY OF EDWIN DROOD

Dickens didn't pour out many stirrup-cups in his lifetime, mainly because he absolutely hated saying good-bye. His close friend, George Dolby, could hardly remember him saying it at all: instead, "his usual parting words to me being 'Good day,' or 'Good night.'" Even Dickens' children reported the same. "My father had such an intense dislike for leave-taking," wrote his daughter Mamie, "we children, knowing this dislike, used only to wave our hands or give him a silent kiss when parting." Of course, it seems astonishing that a man whose life was built on words should be reticent to say any of them. But it's possible that because Dickens was so well acquainted with writing ending chapters he had a stubborn unwillingness to ever face his own. Thankfully, Dickens made one of his few exceptions on June 6, 1870. The morning his daughter Katey left for a trip to London, Dickens surrendered his usual stoicism and embraced her in a parting hug she would never forget. Dickens died two days later.

Swipey

[SWAHY-pee] Drunk.

> *"He's enough to break his mother's heart, is this boy. . . . A muddling and a **swipey** old child," said Miss Wren, rating him with great severity, "fit for nothing but to be preserved in the liquor that destroys him, and put in a great glass bottle as a sight for other swipey children of his own pattern."*
>
> — OUR MUTUAL FRIEND

Etymologically, Miss Wren is being a bit too hard on her father (the parent-child relationship is reversed in the Wren household). Her word for drunkenness, *swipey*, actually denotes a rather mild form of inebriation. *Swipes* was slang for very weak, watered-down beer with an almost nonexistent alcohol content (i.e., a character in *Oliver Twist* figuratively speaks of a boring evening as being "as dull as swipes"). Swipeyness, therefore, was drunkenness in the most innocent extreme—just the sort of drunkenness that Dickens rather liked. His novels are laced with the honest, harmless enjoyment of alcohol—good old English alcohol, such as frothy beers, mulled wines, and fruit-packed punches, which, by and large, are all sipped temperately before a crackling fire in convivial company. If this seems utopian, it was purposeful. It was Dickens' response to another utopian vision circulating in his day, most notably by the Victorian Temperance Movement, who believed that an alcohol-free England would be safer, healthier, and far happier. Dickens found the idea both ridiculous and dangerously myopic, eventually summing its proponents up as a pack of "stupendous fools."

Taking a Sight

[TAY-king·ay·sahyt] A playful gesture of mockery wherein the thumb is put to the tip of the nose with the fingers extended (and often wiggled).

> *Kit soon made himself a very tolerable gardener, a handy fellow within doors . . . even Mr. Chuckster would sometimes condescend to give him a slight nod, or to honour him with that peculiar form of recognition which is called "**taking a sight**."*
>
> **— THE OLD CURIOSITY SHOP**

Today, Mr. Chuckster's gesture would be better known as "thumbing one's nose" or "making a long nose" or even "the five-finger salute"—all of which seem far more appropriate for this nasal gesture than "taking a sight" (something that sounds more eye, than nose related). The discrepancy, however, can be cleared up by looking at the first known reference to nose-thumbing, recorded by the French writer Rabelais in 1532. In Rabelais' wonderfully detailed description, the original gesture had a definite ocular accompaniment—besides the requisite nose-on-thumb, there were winks performed with one eye while the other eye was kept tightly closed as if aiming, or "taking a sight," at the individual one was mocking. But as no one seemed to know the exact reason for this aiming, nose-thumbing in Britain eventually lost its taking a sight connotations and gradually became known as "cocking a snook." Still odd, yes, but much easier to explain: The verb "to cock" means to raise something in an attitude of defiance, while *snook* is likely a variant of snoot or snout, both slangs for the nose.

Tea Gardens

[tee·GAHR-dens] Outdoor dining areas attached to pubs or taverns for taking light refreshments—the outdoor cafés of Victorian London.

---

*Let us turn now, to . . . the Sunday pleasurers; and let us beg our readers to imagine themselves stationed by our side in some well-known rural "**Tea-gardens**."*

— SKETCHES BY BOZ

Despite their prim, pinky-up name, London's nineteenth-century tea gardens were almost exclusively frequented by the lower middle classes. They had, of course, been rather the fashionable fad among the urban elites a century before. Massive tea, or "pleasure gardens," like Vauxhall and Ranelagh in London were the eighteenth-century equivalent to today's amusement parks—places where stylish Georgians could sip tea and stroll through acres of outdoor delights. Their fun, however, was soon spoiled by a few indiscreet lovers who got up to all sorts of hanky-panky in the gardens' sequestered nooks. (And if any of *that* was going to take place among the higher classes, it was going to happen in a country house with a respectable mistress, not among the shrubbery, thank you very much!) And so tea gardens were downsized in the Victorian era, becoming little more than outdoor extensions of English pubs. And where there were pubs, "tea" was a very flexible term—something the tea-garden party in *Sketches by Boz* well knows. Starting with tea, they soon switch to gin, "just . . . to do it up comfortable and riglar arter sitch an as-tonishing hot day!"

Teetotum

[tee-TOH-tuhm] A child's spinning top, originally a Roman gambling device with the letter "T" marked on one of its four sides, standing for the Latin *totum*, "the whole," meaning take the whole winnings.

---

*Wet days, when the rain came slowly, thickly, obstinately down . . . smoking umbrellas passed and re-passed, spinning round and round like so many **teetotums**, as they knocked against each other on the crowded footway.*

— THE CHIMES

One can't read a reference to umbrellas in Dickens' works without paying homage to the queen of umbrella fame—Mrs. Sarah Gamp. The infamously intoxicated nurse in *Martin Chuzzlewit* is so attached to her big, bulgy umbrella, that it became a comical character in its own right, instantly nudging its way into the English language. *Gamp* became, and remains in Britain, a slang for any large, unwieldy umbrella. But Mrs. Gamp's linguistic legacy doesn't end there. A *gamp* can also refer to any disreputable nurse, a reputation largely earned by the original Gamp's proclivity for drinking on duty and amusing herself by rubbing her nose on fireplace fenders.

What Larks!

[whut·lahrks] "What fun!" with *larks* being a ubiquitous Victorian word for "amusement," "frivolity," and "play," particularly of a mischievous nature.

---

*Joe had actually laid his head down on the pillow at my side and put his arm round my neck [and said] . . . you and me was ever friends. And when you're well enough to go out for a ride — **what larks!"***

— GREAT EXPECTATIONS

What larks!—Joe's famously cheery catchphrase in *Great Expectations*— needs no literary introduction. Neither did it need an explanation for Dickens' original readers. They would have known, as Henry Mayhew points out, that "larks" was "a convenient word covering much mischief." *Why* Victorians knew this is a matter of some speculation. Larks could have derived from the Anglo-Saxon *lac* ("sport"), traced further back to the Old Norse *lieka*, "to play"—the root of which persists in playrooms all over the world, thanks to one Danish toy company and its enormously popular toy bricks (hint: they start with "L" and rhyme with grego). It does, however, seem more plausible that "larks" is simply a shortening of *skylark*—a small bird that only sings as it mounts to the sky, thus gaining a reputation for frolicking playfulness. That Dickens preferred this etymology is obvious. Near the end of *Great Expectations* the eternally larking Joe symbolically sits under a blue sky while his playful kindred, "the larks," are "soaring high" above him.

"It Was the Worst of Times"

WORDS FOR BLEAK DAYS AND BAD COMPANY

Barlowed

[BAHR-lohd] Bored by hard facts. Mr. Barlow is the unimaginative, didactic tutor in Thomas Day's popular eighteenth-century children's book, *The History of Sandford and Merton*.

---

*With the dread upon me of . . . being **Barlowed** if I made inquiries . . . I forbore enlightenment in my youth, and became, as they say in melodramas, "the wreck you now behold."*

— THE UNCOMMERCIAL TRAVELLER

The fictional Mr. Barlow came dangerously close to ruining Dickens' lifelong love of learning. As a child, Dickens picked up *Sandford and Merton* and was traumatized by its academically omnipotent figure of Mr. Barlow, who reduced everything in life, "from the consumption of a plate of cherries to the contemplation of a starlight night," to cold, bleak, scientific facts. Dickens would later write a whole ranting essay on the experience, though not before picking a larger pedantic bone in his tenth novel, *Hard Times*—a virtual manifesto against the abuses of Barlowism. Here, Mr. Barlow is recast in the far more intimidating character of Thomas Gradgrind, the harsh schoolmaster, a "man of facts and calculations" who is convinced he can "weigh and measure . . . human nature" with mathematical precision. "Facts alone are wanted in life," he says, and Gradgrind does a pretty good job of grinding out any sentiment, wonder, imagination, or other "destructive nonsense" from his pupils. So good, in fact, he's earned his own adjective—*gradgrindian*—still applied to any heartless adherence to facts.

Barmecide

[BAHR-muh-syd] Disappointingly misleading or illusionary, from a character in *The Arabian Nights* who serves a banquet of imaginary food on empty plates.

---

*Tellson's Bank by Temple Bar was an old-fashioned place. . . . Your bank-notes had a musty odour, as if they were fast decomposing into rags again. . . . Your lighter boxes of family papers went up-stairs into a **Barmecide** room, that always had a great dining-table in it and never had a dinner.*

— A TALE OF TWO CITIES

The Arabian Nights, a classic collection of Middle Eastern and Asian tales, had a profound influence on Dickens as a child. It contained some of the first stories he ever read, illuminating his dreary world with "dear old honest Ali Baba" and his golden adventures. More importantly, Dickens fondly recalled how, through the tales, "all common things [became] uncommon and enchanted to me. All lamps [were] wonderful; all rings [were] talismans." This love for the commonplace would later become a hallmark of Dickens' literary style. And in the preface to *Bleak House,* he makes one of the sincerest critiques of his own work: "I have purposely dwelt upon the romantic side of familiar things." Dickens had been dwelling on it for quite a while, in fact. His first literary "work" (at age nine) was a sort of homage to *The Arabian Nights*. Titled *Misnar, the Sultan of India*, the manuscript has, sadly, not survived, though Dickens sardonically assured his readers that it was received "with great applause to overflowing nurseries."

Barnacleism

[BAHR-nuh-kuhl-iz-uhm] Incompetent and obstructing bureaucracy, named after the governmental Barnacle family in *Little Dorrit*.

---

*The worthy gentleman being not at all clear in his own anxious mind but that the mingling of [hard work] with official **Barnacleism** might produce some explosive combination.*

— LITTLE DORRIT

Aptly named after the most immobile of marine creatures,* the Barnacle family in *Little Dorrit* has parasitically attached itself to every "public post" in the British government, clinging especially hard to the Circumlocution Office—Dickens' famous embodiment of the blatant ineptitude of Victorian bureaucracy. "It being one of the principles of the Circumlocution Office never, on any account whatever, to give a straightforward answer," the Barnacles are here free to indulge their shared love for laziness and purposeful obstruction of progress. Running diametrically opposed to Dickens' hardworking and progressive nature, the infuriating Barnacles were, no doubt, created as literary punching bags for Dickens' own mounting political frustrations. As he wrote to a friend in 1855, writing *Little Dorrit* helped him in "blowing off . . . indignant steam, which would otherwise blow me up."

Barnacle was also period slang for "a good job very easily got." Incidentally, note how every new Barnacle is instantly "secured" a cushy government job without ever working for it.

Bombazeen

[BOM-buh-zeen] A type of silken fabric, usually black and worn during mourning, from the Greek *bombyx*, "silk or silkworm."

> *This celebrated Mrs. Pipchin was a marvellous ill-favoured, ill-conditioned old lady. . . . Forty years at least had elapsed since . . . the death of Mr. Pipchin; but his relict still wore black **bombazeen**, of such a lustreless, deep, dead, sombre shade, that gas itself couldn't light her up after dark, and her presence was a quencher to any number of candles.*
>
> — DOMBEY AND SON

Dickens couldn't have known when he wrote about Mrs. Pipchin, grief-stricken for forty years, in *Dombey and Son* that the passage would soon be a perfect description of the reigning queen of England. But fifteen years later, Queen Victoria seemed to live up to every one of Dickens' words. After the death of her husband in 1861, Victoria plunged herself into full mourning, donning, like a real-life version of Mrs. Pipchin, the same "deep, dead, sombre shade" of black for the same forty years. But what appeared comical in fiction did not translate well in fact. Disappointed by Victoria's excessive grief and deliberate isolation from her own subjects, critical placards started appearing all over the streets of London:

VICTORIA!
Modest lamentation is the right of the dead;
Excessive grief is the enemy of the living.
—Shakespeare

Brimstone and Treacle

[BRIM-stohn·and·TREE-kuhl] The infamous Victorian "tonic"— a preventative cure-all medicine consisting of powdered sulfur (brimstone) mixed with molasses (treacle).

---

*We purify the boys' blood now and then, Nickleby. . . . They have the **brimstone and treacle**, partly because if they hadn't something or other in the way of medicine they'd be always ailing and giving a world of trouble, and partly because it spoils their appetites and comes cheaper than breakfast and dinner.*

— NICHOLAS NICKLEBY

The image of Mrs. Squeers manically shoveling a spoonful of brimstone and treacle down the throat of each student at Do-the-Boys' Hall seems like the sadistic stuff of Dickensian fiction. If only history were so kind. The fact is Victorian children knew all too well what brimstone and treacle was, what it tasted like, and what it did to their bodies. Basically, as Mr. Squeers states, brimstone and treacle was used to regularly clean or "purify the . . . blood"—a common catchphrase of the era for purging the digestive system. Sulfur, acting as a laxative, did this rather effectively. The sweet molasses, on the other hand, was essentially there to mask the sulfur. Its taste, therefore, wasn't all that horrible—the far more unpleasant part of the regimen was the inevitable aftermath in the loo.

Burked

[burkd] Murdered, with the specific intention of selling the body for medical study.

> *"Why, sir, bless your innocent eyebrows, that's where the mysterious disappearance of a 'spectable tradesman took place four year ago." "You don't mean to say he was **burked**, Sam?"* said Mr. Pickwick, looking hastily round.
>
> **—THE PICKWICK PAPERS**

Mr. Pickwick, no doubt, is looking "hastily round" for the face of William Burke, one of the most notorious serial killers in nineteenth-century Britain. With his partner, William Hare, Burke brought a horrifying new level of expertise to the already horrendous Victorian practice of body snatching—secretly digging up corpses to sell to medical schools for anatomy lectures. Usually, men who engaged in this sordid trade (known tongue-in-cheek as *resurrection men*) didn't stoop morally lower than pillaging the local cemetery. Burke and Hare were far less scrupulous. They cut out the middleman (or middle graveyard) entirely and hunted for fresher specimens on the streets of Edinburgh, Scotland. Strangling at least sixteen people, they sold the bodies to a local medical professor before Burke was arrested and executed for the crimes in 1829—though plainly, his surname was still striking fear into the likes Mr. Pickwick almost a decade later. And technically, Mr. Pickwick has a legitimate right to fear. Dickens wrote *The Pickwick Papers* to be set one decade in the past, when, strictly speaking, Burke and Hare were still on the hunt.

Carking

[KAHR-king] Causing distress or worry.

> *Tossing to and fro upon his hot, uneasy bed . . . with no change but the restless shiftings of his miserable body, and the weary wanderings of his mind, constant still to one ever-present anxiety—to a sense of something left undone, of some fearful obstacle to be surmounted, of some* **carking** *care that would not be driven away.*
>
> **— THE OLD CURIOSITY SHOP**

Apparently, Dickens thought *carking* too good a word to use just once in *The Old Curiosity Shop*. Five years later, he would construct a whole character around the term. The villainous and tormenting James Carker in *Dombey and Son* is a walking definition of the archaic verb *to cark,* meaning "to trouble or harass." Secretly piling up troubling burdens on Mr. Dombey and ultimately bringing about his financial ruin, James Carker obviously has a good grasp on the origin of his surname—carking and cark come from Old French *charger*, "to load or burden." But it's Carker's own brother, the gentle John Carker, who seems to bear the literal brunt of this carking weight. Constantly harassed by his stronger-willed brother, John Carker "was not old, but his hair was white; his body was bent, or bowed as if by the weight of some great trouble."

Comfoozled

[kuhm-FOO-zuhld] Exhuasted, overcome.

---

*"Mr. Winkle—you remember him" . . . "Well," said Sam, "he's in a horrid state o' love; reg'larly **comfoozled**, and done over with it."*

— THE PICKWICK PAPERS

The popular theory is that *comfoozled* is yet another one of Dickens' invented words. But given the fact that Mr. Winkle makes an iconic fool of himself throughout *The Pickwick Papers*, it's more likely that Dickens borrowed the term by building upon the older American slang *foozle*, "a man who is easily humbugged or fooled." Either way, poor Mr. Winkle's perennial foolishness and exhausting romance certainly entitle him to both definitions.

Connubialities

[kuh-noo-bee-AL-it-tees] Dickens' polite euphemism for marital arguments, from Latin *conubialis*, "pertaining to wedlock."

---

*"You were speaking about Miss Squeers," said Nicholas, with the view of stopping some slight **connubialities** which had begun to pass between Mr. and Mrs. Browdie, and which rendered the position of a third party in some degree embarrassing.*

— NICHOLAS NICKLEBY

Why do modern marriages have "arguments" while Victorians enjoyed rosy-cheeked "connubialities"? It's the same reason they lived in denial of the dreaded D-word (psst . . . divorce). Victorian marriages, after all, were bound tighter than the tightest corset, a literal till-death-do-us-part contract that took (prior to 1857) an act of Parliament to break. For men, divorce was an expensive nightmare; for women, it was near impossible. From 1827 to 1857, only three women in England were successful in obtaining one—bad odds for the many miserable wives in Dickens' novels. We can almost hear Betsy Quilp let out a sigh in *The Old Curiosity Shop*—she'll have to be terrorized by her "hunchy villain" of a husband for a little longer. But feminist hope springs eternal in another Betsey, Miss Betsey Trotwood in *David Copperfield*. With her private savings, she manages to pay off her abusive husband, who promptly "went to India with his capital" and, by all estimates, got squashed to death while riding an elephant—by far, much easier and more probable than getting a Victorian divorce.

Coverture

[KUHV-er-cher] A Victorian matrimonial law stipulating that a woman's legal affairs and financial obligations were assumed (i.e., covered) by her husband. Dickens uses the word for "marriage" in general.

She had been a slave to poor Nicholas, and had often told him she might have married better . . . with other bitter recollections common to most married ladies, either during their **coverture,** *or afterwards, or at both periods.*

— NICHOLAS NICKLEBY

That coverture was degrading, restrictive, and financially ruinous to women is painfully obvious. One cringes at the casual definition offered for it by William Blackstone, the eighteenth-century legal scholar: "By marriage . . . the very being or legal existence of the woman is suspended." But coverture worked both ways, and women were not its only victims, as Mr. Bumble so awkwardly discovers in *Oliver Twist*. When his wife carries out a bad financial transaction, Mr. Bumble is told "the law supposes that your wife acts under your direction," setting him off on one of the most famous rants in literature:

"If the law supposes that," said Mr. Bumble, squeezing his hat emphatically in both hands, "the law is a ass—a idiot. If that's the eye of the law, the law's a bachelor; and the worst I wish the law is, that his eye may be opened by experience—by experience."

Farm for Children

[fahrm·for·CHIL-druhn] Better known as a "baby farm"—a primitive Victorian child care establishment, notoriously ill managed, where a "baby farmer" was paid to care for unwanted children.

The cholera, or some unusually malignant form of typhus assimilating itself to that disease, broke out in [the] **farm for children**, *because it was brutally conducted, vilely kept, preposterously inspected . . . and a stain upon a civilized land.*

— THE PARADISE AT TOOTING

Baby farming was big business in the Victorian era—an age rife with illegitimate births and the need to dispose of them quickly. And baby farms provided one of the few legal options for doing so. The best were run like foster homes, with a guardian routinely paying for a child's care until he or she could be adopted out of the system. The worst were literal death factories where, for one lump sum, an unwanted child could be left, and where (in cruelly economic terms) it was also in the best interest of the baby farmer to let his or her charges die as quickly as possible, usually by starvation. The baby farm run by Mrs. Mann in *Oliver Twist* seems to be a strange mix of the two. Here, Oliver spends the first eight years of his life with thirty other children, each receiving a sum of 7½ pennies a week for bed and board. But Mrs. Mann pockets most of that while punishing every child for "presuming to be hungry" and dosing them with gin when she can't bear to "see 'em suffer"—making Oliver's miraculous survival at the baby farm perhaps his greatest adventure of all.

Foetid Effluvia

[FET-id·ih-FLOO-vee-ah] Putrid vapors. For Victorians, *effluvium*, from the Latin for "flow out," was, among other things, believed to be a vaporous by-product of rotting organic material.

---

*During some hours of yesterday evening a very peculiar smell was observed by the inhabitants of the court . . . [and] corroborated by two intelligent married females . . . both of whom observed the **foetid effluvia** and regarded them as being emitted from the premises in the occupation of Krook.*

— BLEAK HOUSE

Krook, a somewhat minor character in *Bleak House*, has gone down in Dickensian infamy simply for the way he dies. And it's a real doozy of a death—death by spontaneous combustion—the most sensational death Dickens ever penned. It was a shock-and-awe moment for Victorian readers, who, up until then, would have only heard hazy rumors of the mythic horrors of self-ignition. But here, Dickens bludgeons them with every grisly detail: from the fatty black soot wafting into the street to the charred "broken log of wood" in Krook's favorite armchair. "Oh, horror," Dickens writes, it's Krook himself! It's a masterly crafted scene of suspense, though not everyone was so impressed. Dickens friend, G.H. Lewes, went on the attack, publically decrying Dickens' use of spontaneous combustion as nothing more than unscientific "vulgar error." This stung Dickens to the core; he sounded off his own rebuttals, publishing his personal research into spontaneous combustion and fueling a wider debate that has continued ever since.

Gravelled

[GRAV-uhld] Financially ruined or embarrassed, borrowed from an old nautical slang wherein *gravelled* described a ship that had accidentally run ashore.

---

*I was rather afraid in my own mind that we might have helped to floor you, because there is no doubt that it is our misfortune to do that kind of thing now and then. We don't want to do it; but if men will be **gravelled**, why—we can't help it.*

— LITTLE DORRIT

In *Bleak House*, Guppy also speaks of being "gravelled," though he considers the word "tantamount to knocked over." Either definition works, as financial ruin makes anyone look both run ashore and knocked over—a look that Dickens was intimately familiar with. His father, John Dickens, was gravelled an embarrassing number of times. Feckless and always living above his means, he was an expensive thorn in Dickens' side, though Dickens couldn't help but marvel at his father's tenacity and indestructible spirit in the face of ruin. It was a personality that deserved a place in Dickens' imaginative world, and John Dickens was soon sublimated into the hopelessly indebted character of Wilkins Micawber in *David Copperfield*. A favorite among Dickensian characters, specifically for his untiring optimism (famously distilled in his guiding mantra that "something will turn up"), Mr. Micawber, in turn, got his own place in the English language. Today, improvident positive thinking is commonly referred to as *Micawberism*.

Growlery

[GRUOL-uh-ree] A place of refuge where one goes to vent frustrations.

> *Mr. Jarndyce called me into a small room next his bedchamber, which I found to be in part a little library of books and papers, and in part quite a little museum of his boots and shoes, and hat-boxes. "Sit down, my dear," said Mr. Jarndyce. "This, you must know, is the **Growlery**. When I am out of humour, I come and growl here."*
>
> — BLEAK HOUSE

Mr. Jarndyce goes on to advertise his growlery as "the best-used room in the house." And, seemingly overnight, growleries were being added to the wish lists of many Victorian homeowners. In turn, enterprising architects of the day, like William A. Lambert, started stressing the importance of this new, must-have domestic sanctuary:

> *A study or growlery is just as dear to a man's heart as a boudoir is to a woman's; and the master of the house deserves to have some corner which shall be his very own, whither he can retire when he wishes to read or work, or simply smoke and rest, or receive business visitors, blissfully undisturbed by the rest of the household.*

But for goodness sake, Lambert goes on to say, keep the decoration of the growlery as close "to the masculine heart" as possible, "without any bows or feminine nonsense."

Hipped

[hipd] Depressed, miserable.

> *"You are a little **hipped**, dear fellow," said Eugene; "you have been too sedentary. Come and enjoy the pleasures of the chase."*
>
> **— OUR MUTUAL FRIEND**

Hipped is a contraction of *hypochondria*, though not the hypochondria (the realm of imaginary illness) we're familiar with today. For Victorians, hypochondria was an actual physical affliction, albeit a mysterious one. It was thought to begin in the upper abdomen, just below the ribs, hence the blending of the Greek words *hypo* ("under") and *chondria* ("cartilage" of the breastbone). Here the stomach and other digestive organs could wreak havoc on an unsuspecting Victorian, who, in the medical reasoning of the day, was almost entirely ruled by his or her digestion. When that digestion malfunctioned, noxious "vapors" were believed to be produced, rising up to the brain and turning it into a chemical cesspit of gloomy thoughts and morbid hallucinations. This is the underlining logic behind Scrooge's famous self-diagnosis when confronted with the ghost of Jacob Marley (and his repeated queries on why Scrooge doubts his own "senses"):

> *"Because," said Scrooge, "a little thing affects them. A slight disorder of the stomach makes them cheats. You may be an undigested bit of beef, a blot of mustard, a crumb of cheese, a fragment of an underdone potato. There's more of gravy than of grave about you, whatever you are!"*

Jackanapes

[JAK-uh-nayps] A bold, ill-mannered, and impudent person.

> *The exclamations of delight were uttered to Mr. Bumble: as the good lady unlocked the garden-gate: and showed him, with great attention and respect, into the house. "Mrs. Mann," said Mr. Bumble; not sitting upon, or dropping himself into a seat, as any common **jackanapes** would: but letting himself gradually and slowly down into a chair; "Mrs. Mann, ma'am, good morning."*
>
> **— OLIVER TWIST**

If you're acting like a jackanapes, you've literally gone ape, though the "ape" in jackanapes is probably pure coincidence (albeit a brilliant one). It's more likely that the word meant "Jack from Naples," as *jack-a-napes* was a fifteenth-century term for a tame monkey. Pet monkeys (then known as Jacks) were popularly imported from Naples, Italy, at the time (to give that context, the fabric *fustian,* also imported from Naples, was once called *fustian-a-napes*). The first human, however, to have the ignominious honors of being called a jackanapes was William de la Pole, a fifteenth-century Duke of Suffolk, who made the unfortunately dumb decision to put a pet monkey's chain and collar on his heraldic badge. Was he asking for it, or what?

Jog-trotty

[JOG-traw-tee] Dull and monotonous, as in a *jog-trot*, the slow and steady trot of a horse.

*"And how do you get on, Richard?" said I. "O! well enough!" said Richard. . . . "It's rather **jog-trotty** and humdrum. But it'll do as well as anything else!"*

— BLEAK HOUSE

It's astonishing that Richard should use "jog-trotty" to describe his apprenticeship with Mr. Badger. Mr. and Mrs. Bayham Badger (if their name isn't indicator enough) provide some of the best entertainment value in all of *Bleak House* and working with them would seem to be the comic pinnacle of any career. But therein lies one of Dickens' secret shortcomings (if it was a shortcoming at all): His imagination was too generous, too equitable, to make even the smallest of his characters appear dull. A champion of the commonplace, Dickens was "filled with the first of all democratic doctrines, that all men are interesting," said critic G.K. Chesterton. "He could not make a monotonous man," Chesterton continues, convinced that Dickens could not be a stinting father to any character of his imagination, as Dickens himself was well aware: "I am a fond parent to every child of my fancy . . . no one can ever love that family as dearly as I love them."

King Charles's Head

[king·CHAHRLZ-iz·hed] A personal and annoying obsession. The beheaded figure of King Charles I constantly harasses Mr. Dick, the kindly lunatic in *David Copperfield*, prohibiting him from making any literary progress on his "Memorial."

"I can't make it out," said Mr. Dick, shaking his head. "There's something wrong somewhere. However, it was very soon after the mistake was made of putting some of the trouble out of **King Charles's** *head into my head that the man first came."*

— **DAVID COPPERFIELD**

Dickens knew what it was like to have disembodied heads and voices crowding one's brain. When writing *Martin Chuzzlewit*, he reported that the character of Sarah Gamp kept springing, uninvited, into his mind, constantly whispering to him and making him laugh at the most inopportune times. Presumably this was a normal day in Dickens' creative mind. As far as he could understand it, Dickens was convinced his creativity was not entirely his own: "when . . . I sit down to my book, some beneficent power shows it all to me . . . and I don't invent it—really do not—*but see it*, and write it down."

Knacker

[NAK-er] A slaughterer of old, worn-out horses. From Old Norse *hnakkur*, "saddle," as the occupation originally denoted a horse saddler and harness maker.

---

*I wish I could refer you to the last horse I dined off (he was very tough), up at a **knacker's** yard in Battle Bridge.*

— HOUSEHOLD WORDS

We have to give the speaker credit here—at least he was honest.* Every Victorian Londoner probably dined on horsemeat at least once in his or her life. With 1,000 horses slaughtered each week in London in the mid-eighteen hundreds (for use in fertilizers, horsehair stuffing, and cat food), Dickens was convinced that a large quantity of horsemeat was being pawned off for human consumption—most likely "mixed with the choppings" of diseased cattle and sold "in the disguise of a well-seasoned English German-sausage." It was a common fear, but hypothetically, the only creatures to dine off horsemeat were pampered Victorian cats who often enjoyed a skewer of the stuff (essentially horse-on-a-stick) purchased from the local cat's-meat man. Though even this treatment was too good for Jenny Wren's miserable father in *Our Mutual Friend*: "If you were treated as you ought to be," said Miss Wren, "you'd be fed upon the skewers of cats' meat; only the skewers, after the cats had had the meat."

---

*The speaker is actually a bird, but a rather anthropomorphic one, so same difference.

Mute

[myoot] A professional mourner of Victorian funerals, hired to stand in silent (or "mute") vigil outside the house of the deceased and to walk in front of the funeral procession.

"There's an expression of melancholy in his face, my dear," resumed Mr. Sowerberry, *"which is very interesting. He would make a delightful* **mute***, my dear."*

— OLIVER TWIST

Mr. Sowerberry, funeral director, knows a profitable opportunity when he sees one. He reserves Oliver as a mute for children's funerals; "a mute in proportion," as he puts it, "would have a superb effect." A superbly *expensive* effect is what he really means. Part of the costly and elaborate paraphernalia of Victorian funerals, "mutes come very dear" admits Mr. Mould, the profiteering undertaker in *Martin Chuzzlewit*. In the same book Dickens points out, with his usual knack for spotting irony, that "mutes" usually looked "as mournful as could reasonably be expected of men with such a thriving job in hand." Unwilling to be exploited by this mercenary trade in death, Dickens stipulated in his own will that "I be buried in an inexpensive, unostentatious . . . strictly private" and mute-less "manner."

Nellicide

[NEL-uh-syd] A sentimental killing, after the melodramatic death of Little Nell, the angelically perfect child protagonist in *The Old Curiosity Shop*.

---

*That **Nellicide** was the act of Heaven . . . If you knew the pain it gave me.*

— LETTERS OF CHARLES DICKENS

It's hard to overestimate the popularity of melodramas in the nineteenth century. Originally stage plays running high on emotion, they were the shameless soap operas of their day (complete with wide-eyed stares and cheesy music). They were terribly sappy, totally unrealistic, and oh-so addicting. Dickens, ever the ham himself, took to the melodramatic form with abandon. He reveled in exciting emotions on cue and got quite adept at creating *really* good heroes and *really* bad villains—something Victorians rather appreciated (moral ambiguity was anathema to melodramas). But his crowning melodramatic achievement, of course, takes place in *The Old Curiosity Shop* with the climatic killing off of Little Nell. It oozes sentiment—sentiment we'd consider rather cheap today—but it made grown men cry in its time, and elicited more reader reaction than anything else Dickens ever wrote. Alas, melodramas weren't to last as a viable literary strategy, and modern readers are more likely to side with Oscar Wilde's sentiments: "One must have a heart of stone to read the death of Little Nell without laughing."

Pecksniffian

[pek-SNIF-ee-uhn] Hypocritical, of a self-righteous, self-serving, and heartless nature, behavior originally perfected by Mr. Pecksniff, the puffed-up architect in *Martin Chuzzlewit*.

---

*Mr. Pecksniff . . . seemed to be shrunk and reduced; to be trying to hide himself within himself; and to be wretched at not having the power to do it . . . For a minute or two, in fact, he was hot, and pale, and mean, and shy, and slinking, and consequently not at all **Pecksniffian**.*

— MARTIN CHUZZLEWIT

Why did *Pecksniff* enter the English language so easily? Why did it become such a perfect synonym for hypocrite? The answer has less to do with Mr. Pecksniff's literary legacy than the simple, almost primitive, reason that Pecksniff just *sounds* so hypocritical. It was a triumph of Dickens' linguistic genius to create characters with names that perfectly and phonetically characterize them (i.e., of course Scrooge is a miser, could a *Scrooge* be any different?). And Pecksniff has to be one of Dickens finest-sounding specimens, suggesting a shifty creature who humbly pecks at the ground one moment before haughtily sniffing the air the next, always testing the wind for his next chance to rise in the pecking order. Of course, all of this relies more on Dickens' knack for word association than direct meaning—a formula that, appropriately enough, Pecksniff himself embraces: "Mr. Pecksniff was in the frequent habit of using any word that occurred to him as having a good sound . . . without much care for its meaning."

Petticoat-governed

[PET-ee-koht-guhv-urnd] Henpecked, ruled by the precepts of a nagging wife, with *petticoats* being nineteenth-century female undergarments.

---

*Mr. Calton seized the hand of the **petticoat-governed** little man, and vowed eternal friendship from that hour.*

— SKETCHES BY BOZ

It might seem terribly racy, circa nineteenth century, for Dickens to be mentioning petticoats. They were, after all, a sort of Victorian underwear, and Victorians had a prudish fear of mentioning anything that came close to touching the skin. But petticoats simply didn't inspire enough salacious thoughts to make them particularly taboo. For one, they were worn over an already dizzying amount of female underwear—usually three layers of it. And petticoats were simply long, ruffly skirts, the main purpose of which was to bulk out early Victorian dresses, with poofier dresses requiring multiple petticoats underneath (and apparently, underwear diminishes in sultriness the more one wears). There were, of course, garments that were never mentioned in polite society, at least not without delicate euphemisms. Corsets, for example, were referred to as "stays" and actual skin-touching underclothes were spoken of as "smalls" or "small clothes." The taboo extended to men's clothing as well. The word "trousers" presumably roused too much thought on what lied beneath them, and you'll often find Dickens swapping *trousers* for more genteel terms, like "inexplicables," "inexpressibles," or "unmentionables."

Quarter Days

[KWAWR-ter·dayz] The four days of the English fiscal year (spaced three months apart) in which rents were due and debts were traditionally settled.

---

*It was, in fact, the twenty-fifth of March, which, as most people know to their cost, is, and has been time out of mind, one of those unpleasant epochs termed **quarter-days**.*

— BARNABY RUDGE

Historically, England's financial cycle was rooted in seasonality. Changes from spring, summer, autumn, and winter, which marked important periods in any agricultural society, naturally came to mark its economic structure as well. Specifically, this cycle attempted to solve the timeless problem of unpaid debts by insisting that what was bought in one season was paid for in the next. And so began *quarter days*, those horrible dates for every down-and-out Dickensian character, "moving wonderfully quick when you have a good deal to pay, and marvellously slow when you have a little to receive." Always corresponding with a traditional English holiday, the four "quarter days" were Lady Day (March 25), Midsummer (June 24), Michaelmas (September 29), and Christmas (December 25). Obviously, having to fork over one's rent and possibly go plum broke on a holiday was rather depressing, and the practice eventually died out in England.

Quod

[kwod] Prison, from a misspelled contraction of *quadrangle*—a courtyard within the walls of a prison where inmates were allowed to walk.

---

*The face of the hostess darkened with some shadow of perplexity, as she replied: "Gaffer has never been where you have been." "Signifying in **Quod**, Miss? Perhaps not. But he may have merited it."*

— OUR MUTUAL FRIEND

That some people truly "merited" prison was a firm belief of Dickens. Pioneeringly compassionate on other social issues, Dickens was convinced that the justly imprisoned deserved a just punishment. In short, prisoners should pay for their crimes, usually through hard labor, in what was then deemed the "silent system" of incarceration. Still, the idea of prisoners "silently" working alongside each other didn't sit well with every Victorian. Advocates of the "separate system" believed that crime was highly contagious and that the only way to curb the contagion was by separating criminals in mindless solitary confinement. This is where Dickens drew the line: "I hold this slow and daily tampering with the mysteries of the brain, to be immeasurable worse than any torture of the body . . . those who have undergone this punishment, MUST pass into society again morally unhealthy and diseased."

Rag and Bottle

[rag·and·bot'l] A catchall term for rubbish, more commonly rendered "rag-and-bone," after two common articles of Victorian household waste (see below).

She had stopped at a shop over which was written . . . RAG AND BOTTLE WAREHOUSE. . . . In another [window] was the inscription, BONES BOUGHT. In another, KITCHEN-STUFF BOUGHT. In another, OLD IRON BOUGHT. In another, WASTE-PAPER BOUGHT.

— BLEAK HOUSE

Rubbish, for Victorians, was too good to throw away. Practically every-thing in their world could be repurposed, reused, recycled—and some solid money made on it in the process. This was the period when one man's trash was literally another's treasure. And for no one more than the rag-and-bone man—the iconic scavenger of Victorian waste. With a greasy bag slung over his back, he'd go from house to house, collect-ing (and usually paying a nominal sum for) any unwanted items. This, as his occupational title implied, originally consisted of *rags* (old clothes and textiles) and meat bones from the kitchen. The idea, and profit, lay in selling everything he amassed: the rags sold to paper mills, which recycled old linen into paper, and the bones sold to glue or fertilizer companies. That was the idea, though no one seems to have told Krook, the rag-and-bottle man in *Bleak House,* whose shop is bursting with Victorian trash: where "Everything seemed to be bought, and nothing to be sold."

Rantipole

[RAN-tih-pohl] An ill-behaved and reckless person.

---

*"Well!" cried my sister, with a mollified glance at Mr. Pumblechook. "She might have had the politeness to send that message at first, but it's better late than never. And what did she give young **Rantipole** here?"*

— GREAT EXPECTATIONS

Rantipole might not be a term of endearment for Pip,* but the name does have a somewhat historic pedigree. "Rantipole" was the nickname of the French emperor Napoleon III (1808–1873), who earned the moniker while recklessly waging war throughout Europe. The word itself, however, is an English invention, most likely formed from combining the old dialect word *ranty,* "riotous and wildly excited" with *poll,* "head."

---

*Part of Pip's punishment for being a Rantipole is, of course, getting habitually dosed with "tar water"—something that fills him (and every reader) with dread. Tar water was one of the foulest-tasting medicines of the Victorian era, thought to cure a multitude of ills. As a simple mixture of water and pine tar, it had such a strong, woody flavor (and Pip is given so much of it), that he's usually "conscious of going about, smelling like a new fence."

Scrofulously

[SKROF-yuh-luhs-lee] In a diseased or dilapidated state, based on *scrofula*, a form of tuberculosis known to cause disfiguring ulcers.

Rickety dwellings of undoubted fashion, but of a capacity to hold nothing comfortably except a dismal smell . . . seemed to be ***scrofulously*** *resting upon crutches.*

— LITTLE DORRIT

Victorian London was riddled with scrofulous buildings. Crumbling from age or cheap construction, much of London was literally falling down "like a house of cards," as one visitor to the city noted.* Dickens took notice too. In 1857, a group of houses famously collapsed on Tottenham Court Road, fueling much speculation in the press that Dickens used the event as inspiration for the sensational collapse of Mrs. Clennam's house at the end of *Little Dorrit*. Dickens quickly refuted such claims, stating that the house of Clennam was destined to fall from the very beginning of the story, pointing to early chapters that prophetically described "An old brick house" with a "mind to slide down sideways" and only remedially "propped up" on "some half-dozen gigantic crutches."

*The German nobleman and travel writer, Prince Puckler-Muskau (1785–1871).

Short Commons

[shawrt·KOM-uhns] *Commons*, probably short for "communal meals," were once food allowances given to students at Cambridge University, with scantier meals known as *short commons*.

---

*The evening [meal] arrived; the boys took their places. the master, in his cook's uniform, stationed himself at the copper; his pauper assistants ranged themselves behind him; the gruel was served out; and a long grace was said over the **short commons**.*

— OLIVER TWIST

Two misconceptions surround literature's most infamous food scene: Oliver Twist asking for more gruel. The first is that gruel was some sort of thick, sludgy porridge, the kind that hits your bowl with a disgusting plop. Gruel was far worse than that. Take the aforementioned oatmeal and water it down to a murky, ambiguous gray liquid and you get a better idea of what gruel was (and why we still speak of punishments as *grueling* today). The second is that Oliver's gruel scene is too outrageously cruel to be anything more than another one of Dickens' usual exaggerations. Just tell that to one of the thousands of children who passed through the nineteenth century's primitive welfare system—children like Charles Shaw who described his very Twist-like diet at a Victorian workhouse in *When I was a Child*:

This decoction of meal and water and mustiness and fustiness was most revolting to any healthy taste. It might have been boiled in old clothes, which had been worn upon sweating bodies for three-score years and ten. That workhouse [gruel] was the vilest compound I ever tasted.

Smallweedy

[SMAWL-wee-dee] Nefariously greedy. Mr. Smallweed is the sadistic moneylender in *Bleak House* with a merciless talent for blackmailing and debt collection. He's a Scrooge, as it were, gone hopelessly bad.

Notwithstanding their martial appearance, broad square shoulders, and heavy tread . . . [there were not] two more simple and unaccustomed children, in all the **Smallweedy** *affairs of life.*

— BLEAK HOUSE

Anyone familiar with *Bleak House* can tell you what Mr. Smallweed's "favorite adjective of disparagement" is. Here's one of his obvious hints: "You're a brimstone idiot. You're a scorpion—a brimstone scorpion. . . . You're a Brimstone beast!" Brimstone, meaning "burning stone," an old term for sulfur, had obvious connotations for Victorians. For one, it was enflamed with biblical allusions to hell "which burneth with fire and brimstone." Indeed, Mr. Smallweed is a hideous "Brimstone Baby," far more hellish than human. But brimstone was even more associated with matches, as most nineteenth-century matches were dipped in a brimstone solution that could dangerously flare up with very little friction. Mr. Smallweed seems to be in the same figurative match-making business—dipping desperate, worn-out individuals into debt just for the pleasure of watching them burn. Mr. George says as much when Smallweed comes to call in his debt: "I am not a match for you," says George defiantly—a terribly clever pun that only Victorians would have caught.

Smifligate

[SMI-fluh-gayt] To beat severely.

---

*Mr. Pyke threatened with many oaths to "**smifligate**" a very old man with a lantern who accidentally stumbled in her way— to the great terror of Mrs. Nickleby, who, conjecturing more from Mr. Pyke's excitement than any previous acquaintance with the etymology of the word that smifligation and bloodshed must be in the main one and the same thing.*

— NICHOLAS NICKLEBY

Mrs. Nickleby isn't alone in her etymological ignorance. Even modern scholars aren't fully acquainted with the origin of *smifligate** (or *spifflicate,* as it's more commonly rendered). Coined some one hundred years before *Nicholas Nickleby* was written, the best guess is that it was invented by combining a cacophony of chastising words, such as *stifle, suffocate, spill,* and *castigate.*

---

*The same confusion surrounds Dickens' other beat-up word, *larrup*—an English dialect word meaning to beat, whip, or thrash, used in *Hard Times*: "'By George!' said Mr. Bounderby, "when I was four or five years younger than you, I had worse bruises upon me. . . . There was no rope-dancing for me; I danced on the bare ground and was larrupped with the rope.'"

Sponging-house

[SPUHN-jing-hous] Places of temporary detention for nineteenth-century debtors.

---

*Miss Brass . . . had passed her life in a kind of legal childhood. She had been remarkable, when a tender prattler, for an uncommon talent in counterfeiting the walk and manner of a bailiff: in which character she had learned to tap her little playfellows on the shoulder, and to carry them off to imaginary **sponging-houses**.*

— **THE OLD CURIOSITY SHOP**

Sponging-houses were the worst and most outrageously expensive hotels in Victorian London. Run by government-approved debt collectors, usually out of their own homes, sponging-houses were named for the way they squeezed recently arrested debtors—like sponges—out of their very last pennies, before shipping them off to debtors' prison. They did this by charging the inmates for the very rooms they were forced to occupy. Intentionally overpriced, the best rooms, as Dickens describes in *Sketches by Boz*, went for "a couple of guineas a day"—or approximately $200 today. And Dickens would know. His own father was taken to a sponging-house in 1834—an embarrassing experience that likely inspired "Coavinses' Castle," the gloomy sponging-house "with barred windows" in *Bleak House*.

Stomachic

[STUH-muh-kik] Medicine for an upset stomach.

He was so kind as to squeeze orange juice into [the wine], or to stir it up with ginger, or dissolve a peppermint drop in it . . . although I cannot assert that the flavour was improved by these experiments, or that it was exactly the compound one would have chosen for a **stomachic**.

— DAVID COPPERFIELD

David is lucky: the oddly flavored wine doesn't sound that bad, especially compared to other Victorian tummy remedies, for which easing an upset stomach was far less important than expelling its contents. Enter laxatives, the nineteenth-century answer to almost every ailment—*better out than in* being the prevailing medical thought of the day. For that, the fearfully named "black draught," a mixture of Epsom salts dissolved in senna leaf tea, was always popular. This is the stuff Mr. Smallweed is said to resemble during his frequent needs "to be repeatedly shaken up like a large black draught" (apparently, his old bowels are just as wicked as he is). Though if you preferred your cathartic in capsule form, there were always "blue pills." Containing strong doses of mercury (another effective laxative), blue pills were swallowed across Victorian Britain with almighty enthusiasm. One doctor in Dickens' *Sketches* insists that his sickly patient take one "immediately, or he wouldn't answer for the consequences." The obvious consequences of mercury poisoning wouldn't have occurred to him yet.

Tergiversation

[TER-ji-ver-say-shuhn] From Latin for "to turn one's back." Dickens uses the word in its older, more literal sense: traitorously turning one's back on a former ally.

---

*[John Barsad the spy] knew, as every one employed as he was did, that he was never safe; that flight was impossible; that he was tied fast under the shadow of the axe; and that in spite of his utmost **tergiversation** and treachery in furtherance of the reigning terror, a word might bring it down upon him.*

— A TALE OF TWO CITIES

Dickens usually tells us how to feel about his characters, and John Barsad, a spy in revolutionary France, is "one of the greatest scoundrels upon earth since accursed Judas." So that's pretty straightforward. Far less morally certain for Dickens was the French Revolution itself. Dickens admitted it was a "reigning terror," but he also shared Thomas Carlyle's historic opinion* that terror is the inevitable response of the terrorized. Dickens went on to imbue Carlyle's argument with his own brand of pathos, but stayed true to the basic warning that a bloody revolution awaits any country that mistreats its people: "Crush humanity out of shape once more, under similar hammers, and it will twist itself into the same tortured forms."

---

*Thomas Carlyle's extensively researched book, *The French Revolution,* was Dickens' primary historical reference for *A Tale of Two Cities.*

Toad-eater

[TOHD-ee-ter] A servile fawner, a sycophant.

Poor excommunicated Miss Tox, who, if she were a fawner and **toad-eater**, *was at least an honest and a constant one, and had ever been truly absorbed and swallowed up in devotion to the magnificence of Mr. Dombey.*

— DOMBEY AND SON

It's difficult to catch the brilliance of the above passage unless you know the full, horrible history of toad-eating. Yes, it used to be literal. Eating a toad was an occupational hazard in the quack medicine trade of the seventeenth century. Since miracle cures don't seem to sell without an entertaining demonstration, charlatan doctors would hire an assistant to eat, or pretend to eat, a toad, considered highly poisonous at the time. After waiting for some near-death convulsions, the doctor would save his assistant, just in the nick of time, with a reviving dose of his wonder brew (just a penny a bottle, folks!). Needless to say, anyone who could be coaxed into swallowing a toad had serious submissive issues, which led to the word's later application to all disgustingly servile persons. Which brings us back to Miss Tox, who must have eaten a fair amount of figurative toads in her day. Her surname, after all, is the Latin root for poison (think *toxic* and *toxin*) and Dickens makes it clear in the above passage that, for Miss Tox, "devotion" and "swallowed" are one and the same.

Ugsome

[UHG-suhm] Horrible and frightening, from Old Norse *ugga*, "to dread."

> *There is the belated traveller, going home with bag on back, and stick in hand, who recoils from the **ugsome** devils and long-necked monsters which the moon creates out of the trees and bushes before him.*
>
> **— ALL THE YEAR ROUND**

The ugsome side of life had a powerful hold on Dickens' imagination. Not unlike many Victorians, he had a "horrible fascination" with death, wickedness, and the supernatural; with frightening experiences and spooky tales; with, in short, the irresistible "attraction of repulsion," as he liked to call it. Dickens, after all, grew up during the dawn of the penny dreadfuls—cheap horror magazines that he devoured as a teenager, despite "frightening my very wits out of my head." However no experience for Dickens proved to be as frightening, nor as impactful, as one childhood memory recorded in his short story, "Lying Awake." When he was very young, Dickens believed he saw a goblin, or the image of a goblin, while walking in a country churchyard. The experience "horrified me so intensely," it inspired his first Christmas ghost story, "The Goblins Who Stole a Sexton," featured in *The Pickwick Papers*. This tale, about a group of goblins who haunt a grumpy old gravedigger in a churchyard, would become the rough predecessor to the basic plotline of *A Christmas Carol*.

Unsoaped

[uhn-SOHPD] Unwashed.

---

*The procession started in grand order. The specials surrounded the body of the vehicle; Mr. Grummer and Mr. Dubbley marched triumphantly in front; Mr. Snodgrass and Mr. Winkle walked arm-in-arm behind; and the **unsoaped** of Ipswich brought up the rear.*

— THE PICKWICK PAPERS

Dickens is obviously using "unsoaped" as a comic euphemism for the common rabble, but being an unsoaped Victorian wasn't as common as you might expect. Granted, fully submerging in a hot water bath was a rare (and often impossible) luxury for the average Victorian, but daily, "stand-up washes" were an essential part of their daily routine. Usually performed first thing in the morning, a jug of hot water would be fetched, along with a bowl, cloth, and piece of soap. (Interestingly, the water *had* to be hot, as Victorian era soap did not dissolve or lather in cold water.) Working limb by limb, and paying special attention to the more odor-prone areas, the whole body could be methodically soaped, scrubbed, rinsed, and dried, all while standing up and still modestly clothed in one's nightgown.

Weggery

[WEG-uh-ree] Behavior typical of Silas Wegg, the self-seeking, blackmailing character in *Our Mutual Friend*.

> *"I was in a crushed state of mind at the time. . . . I ever viewed myself with . . . reproach for having turned out of the paths of science into the paths of —"* he was going to say *"villany,"* but, unwilling to press too hard upon himself, substituted with great emphasis—*"Weggery."*
>
> — OUR MUTUAL FRIEND

He might not be the only villain in *Our Mutual Friend,* but Silas Wegg* certainly deserves his own noun. His brand of villainy, after all, is very unique—one that could be defined as a special penchant for sadistic home wrecking. Without any explainable cause, Silas Wegg's chief ambition throughout the novel is to financially bring down the house of the kindly and happy Mr. Boffin: to mercilessly "strip the roof off the inhabiting family like the roof of a house of cards." But as Dickens alludes, Weggery needs no real motive besides the mere "attraction" to "power" and pondering the "spoliation" that it can inflict on others. And dabbling in such powerful "defiance" of happiness "was a treat which had a charm for Silas Wegg."

*For Silas Wegg's more infamous legacy (his wooden leg), see page 198.

"A London Particular"

Bedlamite

[BED-luhm-ahyt] A lunatic, literally a resident of Bedlam—nickname of the Bethlem Royal Hospital in London, England's first psychiatric hospital.

---

*"Why didn't you say who you were?" returned Dick, "instead of flying out of the house like a **Bedlamite?**"*

— THE OLD CURIOSITY SHOP

"Is he mad . . .?" asks a young David Copperfield (the "he" being Mr. Dick, a man haunted by the historic head of King Charles I). It's a question we could ask of countless Dickensian characters—the best of which are all slightly loopy. Miss Havisham hasn't taken off her wedding dress in years and Miss Flite from *Bleak House* keeps twenty-seven caged birds in her small room, one of which is named Spinach. Then there's the "old gentleman" from *Nicholas Nickleby* who has a disturbing taste for "gold-fish sauce" and getting stuck in other people's chimneys. It's "a mad world," says Mr. Dick, and Dickens saw that firsthand. His long-established "attraction of repulsion" made Dickens a frequent visitor to Victorian insane asylums: the worst of which seemed just as mad as its patients, and even the best had "a curious degree of unconscious cruelty." That statement ultimately sheds light on Betsey Trotwood's own benevolent response to David's query, *is Mr. Dick mad?* "Well, his family called him mad, and wanted to lock him up for ever. But I met him, and thought—and still think—he's an extremely sensible, intelligent person. So I offered to take care of him."

Bolting

[**BOHL-ting**] Swallowing food quickly and without chewing. *Bolt* was an old English word for a type of arrow, applied in a figurative sense to things associated with arrow-like speed: as in a lightning bolt, a bolting horse, or, in this case, a very fast eater.

He was about to take another bite . . . when his eye fell on me, and he saw that my bread-and-butter was gone. . . . "You know, old chap," said Joe, looking at me . . . "I've been among a many Bolters; but I never see your **Bolting** *equal yet, Pip, and it's a mercy you ain't Bolted dead."*

— GREAT EXPECTATIONS

Written in 1860, Joe's injunction against bolting food was a bit ahead of its time. A couple of decades later, Victorian health nuts would be swept up in a chewing fad, touting the benefits of prolonged mastication as the surest way to ensure proper digestion and overall health. British Prime Minister William E. Gladstone counted himself among their numbers, making sure to chew each bite precisely thirty-two times, once for each tooth. In America, "The Great Masticator," Horace Fletcher, went a few chews further. He wouldn't swallow until every bite had literally dissolved in his mouth. It took him 720 chews to dissolve a single shallot.

Bow Bells

[boh·belz] The bells of the London church of St. Mary-le-Bow—according to folklore, the distance their sound could travel was said to mark the true boundaries of London.

---

*The offices of Dombey and Son were within the liberties of the City of London, and within hearing of **Bow Bells**, when their clashing voices were not drowned by the uproar in the streets.*

— DOMBEY AND SON

Before Big Ben began bonging in 1859, the Bow Bells of Cheapside were considered to be London's loudest, most iconic peelers. One couldn't even claim the title of "Londoner" if one wasn't born within earshot of them (this, ironically, rules Dickens out). Though the Bow Bells, of course, had their competition. "In almost every yard" in the city "there was a church," says Dickens in *Dombey and Son*, and their "confusion of bells . . . was deafening." Just consult the London-bells nursery rhyme, "Oranges and Lemons," to get a slight idea of how many chimers were once scattered throughout the city. Bow Bells, however, were viewed as something special, even magical. They picked up this reputation from the English folktale of Dick Whittington—a rags-to-riches story in which the Bow Bells play a prophetic part, whispering to Dick that he would one day become lord mayor of London. Dickens rather liked this idea of bells whispering life-changing messages to people. In fact, he would construct a whole story around it: his Christmas tale of 1844, *The Chimes*.

Boz

[boz] The celebrated pseudonym of Charles Dickens, originally more popular and recognizable than the name "Dickens" itself.

Boz was a very familiar household word to me, long before I was an author, and so I came to adopt it.

— THE LIFE OF CHARLES DICKENS

That's Dickens speaking to his friend and biographer John Forster. His *Life of Charles Dickens* (published shortly after Dickens' death) tried to answer the public's innumerable questions about the man who had dominated their literary world. And one of their top queries: how did Dickens adopt the pen name Boz? They had, after all, first been introduced to Dickens through "Boz." His first stories and serialized novels, from *The Pickwick Papers* to *Martin Chuzzlewit,* were marked as either authored or edited "By Boz"—never by Charles Dickens. If this was a strategy by Dickens to surround his first stories in an aura of whimsy and mystery, then the strategy succeeded phenomenally. But why Boz? Dickens told Forster that it originated with Moses, once a pet name for his younger brother Augustus. But since Augustus "facetiously" pronounced Moses through his nose, Moses became "Boses, and being shortened became Boz" (pronounced with a long *o,* as in nose). The name stuck, Dickens borrowed it, and he wisely never told his readers that they were (and we still are) pronouncing it wrong.

Brummagem Buttons

[BRUHM-uh-juhm·BUH-tuhnz] Counterfeit coins.

> *"Commodore!" said the stranger . . . "leave you to pay for the brandy and water,—want change for a five,—bad silver—**Brummagem buttons**—won't do—no go—eh?" and he shook his head most knowingly.*
>
> **— THE PICKWICK PAPERS**

Brummagem is an ancient and alternative name for the town of Birmingham in England, based on local phonetic pronunciations dating back to the Middle Ages. As England's second largest city, Birmingham became a manufacturing hub during the industrial revolution, especially renowned for its metal industries and booming button trade (metal-plated buttons being in particular demand at the time). Naturally, it didn't take Birmingham's brightest to see the criminal opportunities presented by the enterprise, and techniques for making metal-coated buttons were soon employed in the creation of counterfeit copper and silver coins. By the end of the nineteenth century, these illicit "Brummagem button" manufacturers were so flagrantly plying their craft, one visitor to the city noticed signboards audaciously advertising "ALL SORTS OF COPPER COINS MADE HERE."

Cag-maggers

[KAG-mag-ers] Unscrupulous butchers—*cagmag* being an eighteenth-century slang for rotten meat. A character in *Great Expectations* uses the word (with a lisp) in his praise for Mr. Jaggers, the London lawyer:

I became aware that other people were waiting about for Mr. Jaggers . . . [one man was] performing a jig of anxiety under a lamp-post and accompanying himself, in a kind of frenzy, with the words, "Oh Jaggerth, Jaggerth, Jaggerth! all otherth ith **Cag-Maggerth**, *give me Jaggerth!"*

— GREAT EXPECTATIONS

Lawyers certainly got a bad rap in Victorian England, but butchers had it pretty bad too. It was common prejudice that even the best butchers were pathological deceivers, passing off inferior meat for a quick profit whenever they could. The worst meat-sellers haunted every carnivore's imagination, becoming the iconic villain butchers who killed neighborhood cats and dogs (or worse!) for sausages and minced meat. And it didn't help their image that most butchers shopped in one of the seediest spots in London— the Smithfield cattle market—here luridly described in *Oliver Twist*:

The ground was covered nearly ankle-deep with filth and mire; and a thick steam perpetually rising from the reeking bodies of the cattle . . . hung heavily above . . . butchers, drovers, hawkers, boys, thieves, idlers, and vagabonds of every low grade . . . crowding, pushing, driving, beating, whooping and yelling; the hideous and discordant din that resounded from every corner of the market . . . rendered it a stunning and bewildering scene which quite confounded the senses.

Catawampous

[kat-uh-WOM-puhs] Fierce, destructive, devouring.

If you should ever happen to go to bed there. . . . There air some **catawampous** *chawers in the small way too, as graze upon a human pretty strong; but don't mind them—they're company.*

— **MARTIN CHUZZLEWIT**

Like other American colloquialisms recorded in *Martin Chuzzlewit*, "catawampous chawers" was another linguistic souvenir Dickens likely picked up on his first tour of the United States in 1842.* It was, however, one he'd sooner forget. Besides its usual "destructive" meaning, *catawampous* (or *catawampus*) was also an American regional slang for any stinging insect—possibly based on *wampus*, meaning "monster, or hobgoblin." Touring the swamplands near St. Louis, Dickens received his fair share of catawampous attacks, recording in *American Notes* that his "face and nose" were barely recognizable after being "profusely ornamented with the stings of mosquitoes and the bites of bugs."

---

*Disenchanted by England's political shortcomings, Dickens had enormous utopian hopes for America—"the Republic of my imagination." He was famously disappointed. Disgusted by the sight of slavery and its citizens' rustic habits (especially their enthusiasm for chewing tobacco), Dickens returned to England with fresh appreciation: "no tongue can tell, or pen of mine describe" how happy he was to be home.

Catch-em-alive

[KACH-em-uh-lahyv] Flypaper—"Catch-em-alive-Oh!"
being the advertising cry of the city's flypaper sellers.

There was one little picture-room devoted to a few of the regular
sticky old Saints, with . . . such coats of varnish that every holy
personage served for a fly-trap, and became what is now called
*in the vulgar tongue a **Catch-em-alive.***

— LITTLE DORRIT

Although the Victorian Ministry of Health correctly considered London
"a perfect plague of flies," not every resident was so quick to lay out a
sticky piece of Catch-em-alive. Many Victorians grew up with oddly
erroneous schoolbooks instructing them that "the fly keeps the warm
air pure and wholesome by its swift and zigzag flight." Even some sci-
entists of the day, like Dr. Thomas Lamb Phipson, were convinced that
the housefly "tends to purify the air" by its larvae feeding "themselves
upon animal matters which if not disposed of in this manner, would
putrefy and evolve noxious gases into the air we breathe."

Cock-Lane Ghost

[kok-layn·gohst] A notorious London haunting. In 1762, a house in Cock Lane was supposedly laid siege by poltergeist activity (mainly knocking noises heard in the wall), drawing an enormous amount of press and popular speculation before the real "ghost" was discovered: the daughter of the house had hoaxed everyone by making the knocking noises herself.

As it rained after dinner . . . Berry played with them [inside], and seemed to enjoy a game at romps as much as they did; until Mrs. Pipchin [began] knocking angrily at the wall, like the **Cock-Lane Ghost***.*

— DOMBEY AND SON

The mystery of the Cock Lane Ghost was solved in the same year it began, 1762, though Dickens couldn't help but publish his own exposé in the article, "The Ghost of the Cock Lane Ghost," almost one hundred years later. Dickens "had something of a hankering" for ghost stories, said his best friend, John Forster, who was convinced that Dickens "might have fallen into the follies" of actually believing them if not for the "retraining power of his common sense." That common sense proved pivotal in Dickens' journalistic hobby of debunking the rampant fraud of nineteenth-century spiritualism and séances. But if the Cock Lane Ghost taught Dickens anything it was that common sense didn't sell many sensational stories, so he gladly supplied the Victorian market with his own brand of ghostly tales—the spookiest of which include "The Signalman," "To Be Taken with a Grain of Salt," and "To Be Read at Dusk."

Daffy

[DAF-ee] A ubiquitous cure-all medicine for Victorian children, Daffy's Elixir (reportedly invented by seventeenth-century cleric Thomas Daffy) was often laced with powerful, sleep-inducing narcotics.

---

*"What is it?" inquired the beadle. "Why, it's what I'm obliged to keep a little of in the house, to put into the blessed infants' **Daffy**, when they ain't well, Mr. Bumble. . . . It's gin. I'll not deceive you, Mr. B. It's gin."*

— OLIVER TWIST

That gin was winding up in the mouths of babes was rather old news for Victorians. Just look at Hogarth's famous etching *Gin Lane*, created nearly a century before, and note the gin-guzzling infant on the right. From Hogarth's day to Dickens', gin was England's number one problem drug, pumping through the veins of the lower classes in mind-numbing quantities. It was dangerously cheap to make, and practically anything could be distilled into gin, even slops of kitchen waste—a selling point captured in the famously disturbing slogan of London's gin bars: "Drunk for a penny / Dead drunk for twopence / Clean straw for nothing." Dickens wrote a lurid account of these gin bars in *Sketches by Boz*. Known to him as "gin-shops" or "gin-palaces," they were among the only warm, well-lit public places in the city. And London's poor flew to them like moths to a flame—moths caught very young. Among their "ordinary customers," writes Dickens, were "children . . . cold, wretched-looking creatures, in the last stages of emaciation and disease."

Dodman

[DOD-man] A snail. *Dod* is an archaic English word for a bare, rounded hilltop, the etymological reasoning being that "dod men," or snails, carried what looked like small, bare hilltops on their backs.

---

*"I'm a reg'lar **Dodman**, I am,"* said Mr. Peggotty, *by which he meant snail, and this was in allusion to his being slow to go, for he had attempted to go after every sentence, and had somehow or other come back again.*

— DAVID COPPERFIELD

Dickens was no dodman. He knew he was living through what he called, "the moving age," and moved through life with matched speed. But Dickens had his reservations when it came to the ultimate mover of the industrial age—the railway. He bluntly calls it "the indomitable monster, Death" in *Dombey and Son*; a rather appropriate metaphor, as the villain of the book is ultimately killed by a train. Eerily, art nearly imitated life for Dickens in 1865. One of the surviving victims of the infamous Staplehurst Railway Accident, Dickens was traveling to London when most of the train he was traveling on derailed while crossing a bridge. Shaken yet uninjured, he must have vividly recalled how, years before, he praised the slower (yet safer) horse-drawn carriages of his recent past: "What a soothing, luxurious, drowsy way of travelling, to lie inside that slowly-moving mountain, listening to the tinkling of the horses' bells . . . till one fell asleep!"

Dolly

[DOL-ee] Slang for silly, foolish, babyish. Its origin is hazy, though its allusion to a child's baby doll is undoubted.

> *"You are a chit and a little idiot,"* returned Bella, *"or you wouldn't make such a **dolly** speech."*
>
> **— OUR MUTUAL FRIEND**

One Dickensian character would take offense to that sort of language—the incomparable Dolly Varden of *Barnaby Rudge* fame. If you haven't heard of her, don't feel bad. Dolly Varden has certainly slipped in the charts of Dickens' celebrity characters, though ironically, she used to be near the top. The beautiful, coyly flirtatious daughter of Gabriel Varden, Dolly is perennially trimmed in ribbons and has a permanent blush on her cheeks. She is "the very pink and pattern of good looks," says Dickens, "a plump, roguish, comely, bright-eyed, enticing, bewitching, captivating, maddening little puss." In short, Dolly was what every Victorian woman secretly desired to be. And merchandizers were quick to indulge them. There was the Dolly Varden hat—a flat straw cap trimmed with flowers and ribbons (ribbons were *sooo* Dolly)—and the ever-popular Dolly Varden dress. This garment was essentially a throwback to the polonaise dresses of the eighteenth century (known for their poofy backsides) and came in a multitude of bright, flowery prints, though pink was always best. Dolly Varden never failed to crush a heart, or two, when draped in simpering shades of pink.

Double Knock

[DUHB-uhl·nok] A bold, confident knock on a door, technically only performed by one with important business with a household.

> *Mr. Nickleby glanced at these frivolities with great contempt, and gave a **double knock**, which, having been thrice repeated, was answered by a servant girl with an uncommonly dirty face.*
>
> — **NICHOLAS NICKLEBY**

Just leave it up to the Victorians to make door knocking complicated—though in all fairness, they had their reasons. London was distractingly loud, and its household doors got far more action than they see today, thanks to a near constant stream of visitors, tradesmen, postmen, and peddlers. Consequently a whole Morse-like code of door knocking developed to allow households to quickly determine who you were, what you wanted, and if you were worth opening the door for.

The basic knocking rules stood thus: Visitors gave a rapid series of trembling knocks. Servants from other households knocked louder and with a certain flamboyant flair. Modest, hesitant knocks (associated with peddlers) were almost entirely ignored, and tradesmen didn't use the knocker at all, instead ringing their own unique bells, which signaled fresh deliveries to the kitchen. Lastly, postmen also employed a quick and confident double knock, which became something of an acoustic trademark for them, lasting long after the Victorian era. Note the title of the classic 1930s crime novel *The Postman Always Rings Twice*.

Fanteeg

[FAN-teeg] A state of anxiety or worry. Its origins are a mystery, though it's conjectured that *fanteeg* is a whimsical blend of "fantastic" and "fatigue."

"You're a amiably-disposed young man, Sir, I don't think,"
resumed Mr. Weller, in a tone of moral reproof, "to go inwolving
*our precious governor in all sorts o' **fanteegs**."*

— THE PICKWICK PAPERS

While Dickens was writing about fanteegs, Americans were speaking of *fantods*. It's practically the same word with a different spelling, though fantods were linked to more extreme forms of emotional anxiety, almost bordering on hysteria. A marvelously unpretentious word, Mark Twain used it in the *Adventures of Huckleberry Finn*: "These was all nice pictures, I reckon, but I didn't somehow seem to take to them, because if ever I was down a little, they always give me the fan-tods." Dickens never used that spelling, but he certainly had firsthand experience with the fantods. On returning home to England after his six-month trip to America, his five-year-old son Charley sputtered off something to his parents about being "too glad" to see them and then promptly fell into "alarming convulsions" before collapsing from the emotional strain. Consequently, Charley would happily agree with etymologists that *fanteeg* and *fatigue* go hand in hand.

Fisticuffs

[FIS-ti-kuhfs] Victorian slang for boxing, combining the sense of *fisty* (relating to fists) with *cuff*—an archaic English word meaning "to hit or slap, usually with an open hand."

---

*In his college days of athletic exercises, Mr. Crisparkle had known professors of the Noble Art of **fisticuffs**, and had attended two or three of their gloved gatherings.*

— THE MYSTERY OF EDWIN DROOD

Mr. Crisparkle, the gentle boxer cum clergyman in *Edwin Drood*, may have been Dickens' soothing response to a savage fight he personally witnessed in 1860. That year's widely attended and infamously violent bare-knuckle match between John C. Heenan and Tom Sayers directly contributed to the enactment of the Marquess of Queensberry Rules—the first boxing code calling for the mandatory use of padded gloves. Shortly afterwards, Mr. Crisparkle arrives on the literary scene bearing a curiously similar message. Quick to promote the use of civilized "boxing-gloves," Crisparkle's padded appendages are so far from inflicting actual harm they even beam with "softhearted benevolence."

Flummoxed

[FLUHM-uhksd] Greatly perplexed, bewildered, puzzled, though Dickens also employs one of flummox's older meanings of "defeated by trickery."

> *And my 'pinion is, Sammy, that if your governor don't prove [an alibi], he'll be what the Italians call reg'larly **flummoxed**, and that's all about it.*

— THE PICKWICK PAPERS

As far as we know, Dickens was the first writer to print the word *flummox*, though it must have been well established in the vernacular for Dickens to have passed off the joke above. The joke, for those who missed it, is Mr. Weller, in his lovable ignorance, saying that the Italians invented the word. It's a bit like a modern American saying, "What the Chinese call a hamburger." As all Victorians apparently knew, flummox was a born and bred English word. If they knew more than that, they know more than us, as flummox continues to stump etymologists today. It could be related to the English dialect words *flummock* ("to make untidy") or *flump* (the sound of something heavy being thrown down). Another contender is *flummery* ("nonsense") with flummery originally being a sweet dish of gelatinized oatmeal. Aha! Here we strike on something interesting. In the eighteenth-century another gelatinized dessert dish, *blancmange*, was sometimes referred to as "Italian flummery." We might read that as "Italian nonsense." And we might start preparing our humble apologies to Mr. Weller.

Fogles

[FOG-uhls] Handkerchiefs.

---

*"If you don't take **fogles**" . . . said the Dodger, reducing his conversation to the level of Oliver's capacity, "some other [boy] will."*

— OLIVER TWIST

Dodger, in natural accordance with his criminal profession, is speaking of taking *fogles* in the pickpocketing sense. A costly (and conveniently unattached) article of Victorian clothing, silk and lace handkerchiefs were an easy target for London's pickpockets who, rather appropriately, developed the nickname of *fogle-hunters*. Dickens uses the expression in *Oliver Twist*, describing Oliver, the pickpocket in training, as a "young fogle-hunter"—presumably his contemporary readers were well acquainted with the term and needed no further explanation. For the rest of us, the precise origin of *fogle* is somewhat hazy. It could have come from *foglia*, an Italian slang for "pocket" or "purse," though others suggest that fogle came from *vogel*, the German-Yiddish word for "bird." The whimsical logic being that on the streets of Victorian London, handkerchiefs, like little birds, tended to fly out of everyone's pocket.

Footpads

[FOOT-pads] Street robbers, specializing in mugging pedestrians on darkly lit paths (*pad* being an archaic slang for path or road).

It was not unusual for those who wended home alone at midnight, to keep the middle of the road, the better to guard against surprise from lurking **footpads***; few would venture to repair at a late hour to Kentish Town or Hampstead, or even to Kensington or Chelsea, unarmed and unattended.*

— **BARNABY RUDGE**

The places mentioned above were all suburbs on the outskirts of London, so the warning is, do not take long walks through Victorian London at night, unless, of course, you are Charles Dickens. He, for one, had a fearless fascination with taking "night walks" through the seediest neighborhoods of the city, mostly for literary inspiration: for "speculating on the characters and occupations of those who fill the streets." Victorians less brave than Dickens could hire the illuminating services of "link-boys"—street guides that held blazing torches made of *links* (bundles of twigs dipped in pitch or tar). Of course, there was always the fear that link-boys were in criminal cahoots with footpads, purposefully leading their clients into dark alleyways just to snuff out their torches for a dark deed or two. So by and large, it was best for pedestrians to steer clear of nocturnal London altogether, as Dickens was well aware: "After nine, none could walk the streets without danger of their lives . . . robberies and murder were of no uncommon occurrence."

Gonoph

[GON-uhf] Pickpocket, based on variations of the Yiddish word for "thief."

---

*"He won't move on," says the constable, calmly, with a slight professional hitch of his neck involving its better settlement in his stiff stock, "although he [Jo] has been repeatedly cautioned, and therefore I am obliged to take him into custody. He's as obstinate a young **gonoph** as I know. He WON'T move on."*

— BLEAK HOUSE

Jo, the poor street urchin in *Bleak House*, might have only *looked* like a good-for-nothing gonoph, but pickpocketing (and its easy profits) must have been a constant temptation for him. Writing for the Prison Discipline Society in 1839, W.A. Miles reported:

Pickpockets have frequently told me that they never had less than thirty shillings or £2 a week. During their 'harvest', which is the summer season, they have on average £1 a day and one lad who is well-known in the West End abstracts purses with such extraordinary dexterity that he makes no less than £20 a week.*

---

*If true, £20 is an extraordinary sum, as professional office clerks, like Bob Cratchit in *A Christmas Carol*, only earned 15 shillings, or a measly three-quarters of a pound, a week.

Grampus

[GRAM-puhs] An anglicized rendering of *grand-poisson*, French for "great fish," originally applied to dolphins and later to wheezy humans (the idea being that breathless individuals make sputtering sounds, like dolphins blowing out air through their spouts).

After another cold interval, a wheezy little pew-opener afflicted with an asthma . . . went about the building coughing like a **grampus***.*

— DOMBEY AND SON

Dickens had a noted affinity for characters with obstructed airways—even a partial listing of them is rather long-winded: Flora Finching from *Little Dorrit* is everlastingly "short of breath," Mrs. Miff from *Dombey and Son* is a "wheezy . . . dry old lady," Sleary from *Hard Times* has a voice like "a broken old pair of bellows," and Barney, the doorkeeper in *Oliver Twist,* can't breathe at all through his nose, pronouncing *come in* as "cub id." For Dickens, this wasn't so much an adenoid fetish as an act of commiseration. He suffered from miserable, literally breathtaking colds throughout his life. "My chest is raw, my head dizzy, and my nose incomprehensible," he wrote in 1844. Though, as a rather nice consolation for his inconvenience, a breathing disorder has been named in Dickens' honor. The "Pickwickian syndrome," a form of sleep apnea due to obesity, was first spotted in the character of the "Fat Boy" in *The Pickwick Papers,* who falls asleep at the oddest moments. Though attributed to laziness in the book, we now know that the poor thing just couldn't breathe well enough to stay awake.

Hocussing

[HOH-kuh-sing] Drugging a drink for stupefying purposes, a contraction of *hocus-pocus*, the meaningless "magic words" of the charlatan conjuror, used for tricking the unwary.

"The night afore the last day o' the last election here, the opposite party bribed the barmaid . . . to hocus the brandy-and-water of fourteen unpolled electors as was a stoppin' in the house." "What do you mean by 'hocussing' brandy-and-water?" inquired Mr. Pickwick. "Puttin' laud'num in it," replied Sam. "Blessed if she didn't send 'em all to sleep till twelve hours arter the election was over."

— THE PICKWICK PAPERS

If the barmaid had any laudanum left over, you can bet she took a swig herself. Laudanum (a potent brew of opium in alcohol) was too good for the average Victorian to resist. The era's tranquilizer of choice, it calmed, relaxed, obliterated pain, and gave most of its drinkers the best sleep of their lives. "There's nothin' so refreshin' as sleep," says Sam in *The Pickwick Papers,* referring to a servant girl who downs an "egg-cupful o' laudanum" before bed. How young this servant girl is didn't seem to matter. Even babies were habitually treated to knockout doses of laudanum. A whole slew of opiate-based "medicines" for quieting infants were marketed to nineteenth-century mothers. They all promised the Victorian parental ideal (that children should be seen, not heard) and many were frightfully blunt about it, with names such as "Dalby's Calmative," "Winslow's Soothing Syrup," and the rather unsettling "Street's Infant Quietness."

Horse Guards' Time

[hawrs·gahrds·tahym] The exact, precise time. The clock over the Horse Guards Parade in London was thought to be the most accurate and reliable clock in the city before Big Ben.

Thus rumour thrives in the capital. . . . By half-past five, post meridian, **Horse Guards' time**, *it has even elicited a new remark from the Honourable Mr. Stables.*

— BLEAK HOUSE

Punctuality was a quasi-religion for Victorians. Home clocks and pocket watches were cheaper than ever and time was the one democratic gift: Everyone got their equal share, though the virtuous could do more and be more, simply by being punctual. The philosophy found an enthusiastic convert in Dickens as his daily routine, summarized in 1867, attests:

I rise at seven; at eight I breakfast; until ten I walk or ride and read the morning papers; at ten precisely I go to my desk and stay there till two, and if particularly in the vein keep at it until four. Then I take the open air for exercise, usually walking. At six I sit down to dinner . . . during which time I discuss domestic matters with my family or entertain such friends as may honor me with their visits. This, the great occasion of the day, over, I retire to my study . . . and exactly at twelve I extinguish my lights and jump into bed. So rigid is my conformity to this method of work that my family say I am a monomaniac on the subject of method.

Kye-bosk

[KAHY-bosk] Dickens' slang rendering of *kibosh*. Its origin and precise meaning is now a mystery, though the Victorian phrase "to put the kibosh on (something)" still means to dispose of something or someone in a crushing defeat.

---

*"What do you mean by hussies?" interrupts a champion of the other party, who has evinced a strong inclination throughout to get up a branch fight on her own account ("Hooroar," ejaculates a pot-boy in parenthesis, "put the **kye-bosk** on her, Mary!").*

— SKETCHES BY BOZ

Kibosh has long been considered a Dickensian *neologism*. From the Greek for "new word," a neologism, in literature, is usually defined as a completely new word or expression never before seen in print. In this case, kibosh first saw the literary light of day in *Sketches by Boz*—or so the story has been told. It's also been said that kibosh is but a puff of air in the enormous balloon that is Dickens' neological legacy, with hundreds of now common words credited to his first use or invention. The list is a ponderous one, including such specimens as *boredom, rampage, butter-fingers, footlights, fairy story, confusingly, natural-looking,* and *snobbish*. Regrettably, it's time to burst that balloon. Blame it on technology and the better research it affords, but many of Dickens' neologisms have now been nullified, with researchers finding slightly older uses of each word in other printed sources.* Talk about putting the old kibosh on them forever!

---

*For Dickens' neologisms that have withstood the test of time, see Flummoxed and Sawbones on pages 110 and 129.

London Particular

[LUHN-duhn·per-TIK-yuh-ler] The iconic fog (though more like smog) of Victorian London.

> *I asked him [Mr. Guppy] whether there was a great fire anywhere? For the streets were so full of dense brown smoke that scarcely anything was to be seen. "Oh, dear no, miss," he said. "This is a **London particular**."*
>
> — BLEAK HOUSE

Dense fogs have been recorded hovering over London since its Roman occupation. Topographically, London is surrounded by marshland and sits within a slight basin in the Thames River Valley—perfect conditions for attracting and trapping fog. Add air pollutants into the mix and fog itself becomes the trap; the trap of coal smoke from millions of chimneys in the nineteenth century engulfed Victorian London in a near constant "sooty spectre" that atmospherically defined Dickens' city. At a distance, London looked like a veritable "city in the clouds" (*Martin Chuzzlewit*). On closer inspection, it was a city laden with sulfuric acid (another by-product of coal fires), which turned its fogs toxic shades of pale green, brown, and pea-soup yellow, giving rise to the term "pea-souper" for the era's heaviest fogs. It was just the sort of industrial weather that perfectly suited the Dickensian world—gloomy, melodramatic, and mysteriously cozy. "The very atmosphere declared him," said the novelist George Gissing, "if I gasped in a fog, was it not Mr. Guppy's 'London particular'?"

Lummy

[LUHM-ee] First rate, originally part of the longer interjection *Lor' lummy*, a Cockney contraction of "Lord love me," used to express surprise or great interest.

> *To think of Jack Dawkins—**lummy** Jack—Dodger—the Artful Dodger—going abroad for a common [crime]. . . . Oh why didn't he rob some rich old gentleman . . . and go out as a gentleman, and not like a common prig, without no honor nor glory!*
>
> — OLIVER TWIST

One gets the impression that Dickens created the Artful Dodger just for his phenomenal vocabulary. The Dodger speaks in fluent and frequent "cant"—the street language of the suave Victorian criminal—and Oliver Twist finds it difficult to keep up linguistically. "I don't know what that means," Oliver constantly says, cueing the many eye-rolls from his new criminal family of prostitutes, pimps, pickpockets, and burglars. So let's help Oliver out with the basics: One might rob a *heavy-swell* ("a well-dressed man") with the aid of *barkers* ("pistols") and get some *blunt* ("ready money"), but be wary of *beaks* ("policemen") or you might end up *lagged* ("transported to Australia"). Interestingly, one cant term that Dickens left out of the book was *twisted*, meaning "hanged." This was probably purposeful, as Oliver's surname itself is likely an allusion to the word. After all, most Victorian boys who started on the path of criminality would soon find their neck *twisting* in a hangman's noose.

Mudlarks

[MUHD-lahrks] Scavenger children, particularly those who scrounged the muddy shores of the river Thames searching for items of value.

> The school at which young Charley Hexam had first learned from a book . . . was a miserable loft in an unsavoury yard . . . [filled with] unwieldy young dredgers and hulking **mudlarks**.
>
> — OUR MUTUAL FRIEND

The river Thames was the last recourse for the miserably poor in nineteenth-century London. An open sewer and dumping ground for the last vestiges of Victorian rubbish, the Thames was a sludgy cesspool at low tide, reeking with potential for every desperate mudlark. With a rake, or just their hands, they dug frantically through the cold mud, finding the odd bit of coal, rope, or a rusty nail—anything they could sell into the era's ravenous recycling market. On very rare occasions, they might happen upon a valuable trinket dropped by a passing boat, but that was the stuff mudlark dreams were made of. The nightmare upon the river, though, was not in mudlarking, but in the scavenging job performed by Jesse Hexam and his daughter in *Our Mutual Friend*. They earn a grislier living by dragging the river for dead bodies, quickly robbing them of any valuables before another desperate "waterman" has a chance to do the same. That their livelihood was greatly supplemented by the frequent river suicides of the nineteenth century is undoubted. The Thames was the last recourse for the miserable Victorian in more ways than one.

Myrmidons of Justice

[MUR-mi-dons·uhv·JUHS-tis] A highfalutin slang for the police, based on a warrior people in Greek mythology (known as the Myrmidons) who loyally fought with Achilles in the Trojan War.

---

*When the day came round for my [Pip's] return to the scene of the deed of violence, my terrors reached their height. Whether **myrmidons of Justice**, specially sent down from London, would be lying in ambush behind the gate? Whether Miss Havisham . . . might rise in those grave-clothes of hers, draw a pistol, and shoot me dead?*

— GREAT EXPECTATIONS

Whereas Pip was frightened by the police, Dickens was fascinated by them. In his boyish admiration, every policeman had the makings of a "guardian genius . . . bringing his shrewd eye to bear on every corner" of London's criminal underworld. At thirty-four, Dickens even entertained the idea of switching careers entirely and becoming a police magistrate—presumably during a period of severe writer's block. In the end, however, he chose to champion London's newly formed Metropolitan Police force (then suffering a public image problem) by writing numerous articles in their defense and, more memorably, by peppering *Bleak House* with the keen deductions of Inspector Bucket—one of the first murder-mystery detectives in English literature.

Near as a Toucher

[neer·az·ay·TUH-cher] As near as possible without actually touching.

> "I can't say I know where it is, for I come from Winchester and am strange in London." "Only round the corner," said Mr. Guppy. "We just twist up Chancery Lane, and cut along Holborn, and there we are in four minutes' time, as **near as a toucher**."
>
> — BLEAK HOUSE

Mr. Guppy knows he's being a bit facetious. Hardly anything in Victorian London was as near as a toucher. The largest city in the world at the time, London, according to Dickens, was a massive labyrinth of "streets, streets, streets," sprawling and stretching "far away towards every point of the compass." Some, like Florence in *Dombey and Son*, were "stunned" and frightened "by the noise and confusion" of this metropolitan maze. Dickens, of course, delighted in it. London was a cinematic experience for him. He spoke of it as his personal "magic lantern" (a sort of slide projector) that sent up an endless revolution of new pictures, comic or pathetic, that he could focus into memorable fiction. Without these pictures, without the energetic soundtrack of London's "roaring streets," Dickens felt his own creativity dangerously dimming. "I can't express how much I want [London's streets]," he desperately wrote to a friend while temporarily living in Switzerland, "the toil and labor of writing, day after day, without that magic lantern, is IMMENSE!!"

Pantechnicon

[pan-TEK-ni-kon] A famous London warehouse, bazaar, and furniture dealer.

---

*Mr. and Mrs. Veneering were bran-new people in a bran-new house in a bran-new quarter of London. Everything about the Veneerings was spick and span new. All their furniture was new . . . they themselves were new, they were as newly married as was lawfully compatible with their having a bran-new baby, and if they had set up a great-grandfather, he would have come home in matting from the **Pantechnicon**, without a scratch upon him.*

— OUR MUTUAL FRIEND

That the Veneerings could purchase a great-grandfather from the Pantechnicon was only a slightly exaggerated joke. With a Greek name roughly translating to "all art," it seemed as if anything could be found within its colossal walls. Built in 1830 and spanning about two acres of ground in Belgrave Square, it was "the largest, the safest, and the most fireproof warehouse in the metropolis," according to the *Times.** Dickens even found a carriage for sale there, or, as he put it, "some good old shabby devil of a coach—one of those vast phantoms that hide themselves in a corner of the Pantechnicon."

---

*Ironically, the Pantechnicon did burn down in 1874, though its large carriages for transporting furniture had been such a ubiquitous sight throughout London that moving vans in Britain are still referred to as *pantechnicons*.

Queer Street

[kweer·street] The imaginary home of Victorian losers in life, especially financial losers.

> *"Well, gentlemen," said Mr. Pell . . . "I don't wish to say anything that might appear egotistical, gentlemen, but I'm very glad, for your own sakes, that you came to me; that's all. If you had gone to any low member of the profession . . . you would have found yourselves in **Queer Street** before this."*
>
> **— THE PICKWICK PAPERS**

First, to clear the air (which we sense has thickened on this page). *Queer*, as slang for homosexual, would have been totally unknown to Dickens. Though that's not to say that *queer* didn't have its Victorian adaptability. From a German word for "oblique, off-center," it absorbed an infinite number of meanings: anything strange, odd, eccentric, unwell, bad, wrong, or improper could be considered *queer*. So it wasn't that much of a stretch to speak of people in difficult financial straits as figuratively living on "Queer Street." But it's just enough of a stretch to puzzle etymologists today. Nonetheless, one amusing theory continues to circulate: It states that Queer Street is a corruption of Carey Street in London, formerly the location of the city's bankruptcy court—and who would want to end up there? It's a delightful, though dubious connection as the bankruptcy court wasn't moved to Carey Street until 1840, about thirty years after the figurative use of "Queer Street" was first recorded.

Rip

[rip] A wicked, unprincipled man; a slang contraction of *reprobate*

I never come across such a vagabond, and my mate says the same. Broke his poor wife's heart, turned his daughters out of doors, drove his sons into the streets. . . . Hope for HIM, an old **rip***! There isn't too much hope going.*

— NICHOLAS NICKLEBY

The fact that Dickens, in later life, was somewhat of an old rip himself and that he could, at his worst moments, be selfish, bad-tempered, and unforgiving is a fact that has always made his admirers uneasy. He became so profoundly and perfectly immortalized, even in his lifetime, it's easy to forget he was once a mere mortal, and a flawed one at that. As Dickens told the Russian novelist Dostoevsky in 1862, it was an uncomfortable fact that he personally struggled with as well:

He told me that all the good simple people in his novels, Little Nell, even the holy simpletons like Barnaby Rudge, are what he wanted to have been, and his villain were . . . what he found in himself. . . . There were two people in him, he told me: one who feels as he ought to feel and one who feels the opposite. From the one who feels the opposite I make my evil characters, from the one who feels as a man ought to feel I try to live my life. Only two people? I asked.

Rookery

[ROO-kuh-ree] The Victorian word for an urban "slum." Rookeries were originally the nesting places of rooks (birds in the crow family) who build large, densely clustered colonies in treetops—a perfect metaphor for overcrowded human dwellings.

We will make for Drury–Lane, through the narrow streets and dirty courts which divide it from Oxford-street . . . best known to the initiated as the "Rookery."

— SKETCHES BY BOZ

Hold tight to your reticules, Dickens is leading us through St. Giles, one of the absolute worst neighborhoods in Victorian London. As Dickens says, it wasn't just one of the city's rookeries (and there were many), St. Giles was *the* Rookery—the place where poverty and humanity couldn't possibly sink any lower. Centrally situated in London (and uncomfortably close to richer neighborhoods), St. Giles and its environed slums epitomized, for Dickens, everything that was wrong with the nineteenth-century social system: mainly that higher-class Victorians had a horrible habit of ignoring poverty, even when it literally abutted their backyards. It's just the sort of willful ignorance that prevents David Copperfield's immensely practical aunt from understanding why his childhood home is called "the Rookery": "In the name of Heaven," she says, "why Rookery? . . . Cookery would have been more to the purpose, if you had had any practical ideas of life."

John Henry Sherburne, American author of *The Tourist's Guide*,1847.

Roopy

[ROO-pee] Hoarse, from Scottish *roup*, "to shout."

---

*"Now, I'll tell you what, young Copperfield," said he: "the wine shall be kept to wet your whistle when you are story-telling." I blushed at the idea, and begged him, in my modesty, not to think of it. But he said he had observed I was sometimes hoarse—a little **roopy** was his exact expression—and it should be, every drop, devoted to the purpose he had mentioned.*

— DAVID COPPERFIELD

Young Copperfield indeed! David is only "between eight and nine years old when offered this wine—as casually as if he were an adult In general, Victorians were quite lackadaisical when it came to child hood drinking. It certainly wasn't uncommon to see childrer frequenting pubs in and around London. Dickens himself remembered waltzing into one when he was just "a little fellow" and proudly asking the barman for the "best—the VERY best—ale" on the premises. Even hard liquor was readily available to children. One visitor to the city was struck by the number of young customers in London's gin shops "each a small pitcher or bottle in one hand, waiting their turn . . . with looks of greedy anxiety." Squalid scenes like this became a rallying point for the nineteenth-century temperance movement, which pressured Parliament to enact the Licensing Act of 1872, prohibiting the sale of alcohol to "any person apparently under the age of sixteen years."

Sawbones

[SAW-bohnz] Sam Weller's slang coinage for a surgeon—Victorian surgeons being infamously adept at cutting off limbs with their amputating saws.

---

*"What's a **Sawbones**?" inquired Mr. Pickwick, not quite certain whether it was a live animal, or something to eat.*

— THE PICKWICK PAPERS

How any Victorian could have laughed at that joke is astonishing. Before 1846 (and the arrival of anesthesia), surgery in nineteenth-century Britain hadn't a smidge of comedy about it. There was no real sterilization, no replacement for blood lost, and the best pain relief a patient could hope for was a small dose of opium and being pinned down to the operating table with numbingly tight straps. Death by shock or infection was a usual risk for going under the Victorian knife (or saw). Nevertheless, Dickens continued to pile on the sawbone jokes in *The Pickwick Papers,* especially with the dodgy medical students Ben Allen and Bob Sawyer—"a parcel of young cutters and carvers of live people's bodies." Dickens' tune, however, would soon change. In 1841, he underwent a surgery himself (the squeamish should turn away now) to remove a painful fistula from his anus. The surgery was "terrible, frightful, horrible," and Dickens refused to say any more, though, unsurprisingly, he didn't crack many surgical jokes after that. "Experientia does it," as Mrs. Micawber would say.

Scrowdging

[SKROUD-jing] Crushing, squeezing, crowding; likely a corruption of the old English word *scruze*, "to squeeze or compress."

> *At last they got to the theatre . . . and in some two minutes after they had reached the yet unopened door, little Jacob was squeezed flat, and the baby had received divers concussions . . . and Kit had hit a man on the head with the handkerchief of apples for "scrowdging" his parent with unnecessary violence.*
>
> **—THE OLD CURIOSITY SHOP**

Smitten with the sound of this obscure and wonderfully expressive word, Dickens wrote about "scrowdging" in *The Old Curiosity Shop* only three years before using it to create one of his most memorable characters. Scrooge, from *A Christmas Carol*, has a surname (and a personality) linguistically linked to scrowdging, or *scrouging*, as it's more commonly spelled.* Scrouging has a variety of squeezing definitions, but Dickens, of course, would hit upon the best: "he was a tight-fisted hand at the grindstone, Scrooge! a squeezing, wrenching, grasping, scraping, clutching, covetous old sinner!"

---

*Another theory is that "Scrooge" is simply a whimsical corruption of *screw*—a nineteenth-century slang for a miser. Indeed, Scrooge is called "a wicked old screw" in the story. But as *screw* and *scrouging* are thought to share the same linguistic root, both are technically correct.

Sharper

[SHAHR-per] A swindler, a variation on *sharker* (as in card shark or loan shark) and likely deriving from the German *schurke*, "rascal, scoundrel."

> *Tom's evil genius did not lead him into the dens of any . . . ring-droppers, pea and thimble-riggers, duffers, touters, or any of those bloodless **sharpers**, who are, perhaps, a little better known to the Police.*
>
> **— MARTIN CHUZZLEWIT**

If you're not up on the latest Victorian street scams, here's a crash course on what "man-traps" to avoid in nineteenth-century London. A "ring-dropper" was a con artist who pretended to find a golden ring on the street and quickly sell it to the first gullible person he could convince of its value—which, of course, was none at all, as the ring in question was only brass at best. Next, "pea and thimble-riggers" were gambling tricksters, practicing a variation on the old, unwinnable game of finding a ball under quickly shuffled cups (in this case, a pea under three thimbles). "Duffers" sold counterfeit goods, *duff* being a British dialect word for anything worthless. And lastly, "touters," from the Middle English *tuten*, "to peer," were the spies and scouts of thieves whose sole job was to lure more business to every swindler in London. To make this work, touters had to be expert salesmen, advertising their boss's scams in an irresistible cloak of innocence. In fact, we still use this Dickensian language today: the common phrase "touting its benefits" continues to apply to anything highly praised or promoted.

Slangular

[SLANG-yuh-ler] Pertaining to slang words.

---

*Little Swills . . . Being asked what he thinks of the [court] proceedings, characterizes them (his strength lying in a **slangular** direction) as "a rummy start."*

— BLEAK HOUSE

There's no knowing for sure what Little Swills actually meant by "a rummy start." *Rummy* (often shortened to *rum*) was one of the most flexible slang words in the Victorian lexicon. Ranging in meaning from anything odd and peculiar to anything particularly fine and excellent, *rum* limberly shifted its definition according to its context. For example, a "rum chant" was a good song, while a "rum customer" was someone who couldn't be trusted. That said, Little Swills' "rummy start" is likely synonymous with *rum go*, meaning "a strange incident or affair." Dickens used the term "rum go" in *The Pickwick Papers*, similarly summing it up as "a very extraordinary thing!"—no doubt, a definition that could easily be applied to the strange court proceedings Little Swills just witnessed in *Bleak House*.

Slap-bang

[slap-bang] A cheap London eating house.

---

*Their incomes were limited, but their friendship was unbounded.
They lived in the same street, walked into town every morning
at the same hour, dined at the same **slap-bang** every day, and
revelled in each other's company every night.*

— SKETCHES BY BOZ

If you're hankering for a quiet meal in Victorian London, don't go to a
slap-bang! Like a noisy diner with a no-nonsense staff, slap-bangs were
named after the manner in which dishes were unceremoniously plopped
down at the table—with a slap and a bang—speed being their major
selling point. It certainly wasn't comfort. Customers were squeezed into
"boxes"—tall wooden booths with hard, narrow seats—and the table-
cloths were, as Dickens jokes, "geographical" (with so many stains, they
looked more like "maps of the world"). But the cheapness of these eating
houses was a great attraction to London's working classes, who were
more than willing to put up with a little dish-slapping to enjoy an afford-
able meal out. In *Bleak House*, Guppy's substantial "Slap-Bang" dinner
for three was a bargain at 42 pence (around $30 in modern equiva-
lence)—a hearty meal of meat, potatoes, bread, and cheese, washed
down with beer and four glasses of rum. And when it came to tipping,
the bargains just got better: one penny per person, no matter what the
final bill ran to. Slap away, dear servers . . .

Slavey

[SLAY-vee] A lowly child servant, one who performs menial work with obvious connotations of "slave."

---

*I am to be found at home every morning. Two distinct knocks, sir, will produce the **slavey** at any time.*

— THE OLD CURIOSITY SHOP

Servants were the must-have commodities of the Victorian age. Rich households had more of them, poorer households had fewer, but few dreamt of doing without them entirely, even if they had to settle for a slavey. Politely known as a *maid-of-all-work,* slaveys were the work-horses of their world, seriously overworked and underpaid (if paid at all, hence the idea of "slave"). Bed and board was often the only remittance for their backbreaking work and *that* usually meant sleeping in a basement kitchen and eating the family's scraps. *Have a little pity* was effectively Mrs. Beeton's message in her popular household manual: "The general servant, or maid-of-all-work, is perhaps the only one of her class deserving of commiseration: her life is a solitary one, and, in some places, her work is never done." Dickens could do better than that. In *The Old Curiosity Shop*, he depicted the drudging life of a slavey so well that she comes awkwardly close to stealing the sympathetic limelight away from the book's real child heroine, Little Nell.

Stews

[stooz] Brothels. The word harkens back to medieval bathhouses where patrons would soak (i.e., *stew*) in unisex baths and, no doubt, did a little bit more under the surface.

---

*The girl's life had been squandered in the streets, and the most noisome of the **stews** and dens of London.*

— OLIVER TWIST

Like a proper Victorian, Dickens was careful to avoid any direct reference to sexuality in his novels. Anything that "could bring a blush into the most delicate cheek" was heavily censored (hence using the archaic and innocuous term *stew* instead of brothel). We don't know how Dickens felt about having to perform this linguistic circumlocution, though prostitution hardly brought a blush to his own cheek. On the contrary, he took an active interest in the plight of prostitutes, so many "friendless, forlorn, and unpitied" by the society that helped to create them. And in 1847, with the financial backing of a wealthy friend, Dickens opened a small recovery home for "fallen women." He called it "Urania Cottage," proving that Dickens was a master wordsmith even in the naming of charities. *Urania* was one of the epithets of Venus, the Roman goddess of love. But whereas Venus was equated with sexual love, Urania represented a higher celestial love. In short, Urania is Venus transformed and perfected. And while Urania Cottage didn't exactly turn out celestial goddesses, it did help some thirty women start new lives in Australia, South Africa, and Canada.

Stumpy

[STUHM-pee] Money, of unknown origin, but presumably deriving from the old idiom, "to pay on the stump," meaning to pay for something immediately, without delay.

---

*Mr. Barker had not officiated for many months [as coachman], when . . . his active mind at once perceived how much might be done in the way of . . . shoving the old and helpless into the wrong buss, and carrying them off, until, reduced to despair, they ransomed themselves . . . and forked out the **stumpy**."*

— SKETCHES BY BOZ

Mr. Barker isn't the only one with the idea. According to Dickens, pedestrians were being kidnapped by omnibus drivers all over London. In theory, omnibus coaches (nineteenth-century horse-drawn ancestors to modern buses) only had space for about twelve passengers—packing more in was the prerogative of every profiteering coachman. "Any room?" asks one unwary pedestrian of an omnibus driver in *Sketches by Boz,* "'Plenty o' room, sir' . . . rejoins the cad, shoving him in, and slamming the door." Elsewhere in the *Sketches*, a driver makes the candid boast that "he can chuck an old gen'lm'n into the buss, shut him in, and rattle off, afore he knows where it's a-going to." Such acrobatic feats, Dickens wryly adds, are frequently performed on the streets, "to the infinite amusement of every one but the old gentleman concerned, who somehow or other, never can see the joke of the thing."

Twigging

[TWI-ging] Observing, inspecting. Technically, the origin of *twigging* is uncertain, though it does share a suggestively similar sound to the Irish/Scottish word *tuig*, "to understand."

> *"They're a twiggin' of you, Sir,"* whispered Mr. Weller. *"**Twigging** of me, Sam!"* replied Mr. Pickwick . . . on looking up, [and becoming] sensible of the pleasing fact, that all the four clerks . . . were minutely inspecting the figure and general appearance of the supposed trifler with female hearts, and disturber of female happiness.
>
> **— THE PICKWICK PAPERS**

These four twigging clerks have got nothing on Dickens, whose powers of observation were legendary in his day. "We have heard," wrote a mid-nineteenth-century critic, "that he can go down a crowded street, and tell you all that is in it, what each shop was, what the grocer's name was, how many scraps of orange-peel there were on the pavement. His works give you exactly the same idea." To Dickens' contemporaries, this remarkable talent for capturing detail was nothing less than artistic genius, the same ability shared by painters and sketch artists—making the title of his first book, *Sketches by Boz*, an intensely appropriate one. Today we might be more inclined to say that Dickens possessed a photographic memory. We would say it, that is, if Dickens hadn't beat us to the idea: "I walked . . . and made a little fanciful photograph in my mind. . . . I couldn't help looking upon my mind as I was doing it, as a sort of capitally prepared and highly sensitive plate."

Walk-ER

[wawk-ER] An expression of utter disbelief, usually pronounced in a drawn out *Waa—alker!*

> *"Do you know the Poulterer's, in the next street but one, at the corner¿ . . . Do you know whether they've sold the prize Turkey that was hanging up there¿" [said Scrooge] . . . "It's hanging there now," replied the boy. "Is it¿" said Scrooge. "Go and buy it." "**Walk-ER!**" exclaimed the boy.*

— **A CHRISTMAS CAROL**

You go, boy! Finally, the comic justice we've been waiting for in *A Christmas Carol*. Scrooge practically calls everyone a "humbug" at the start of the story, so it's only fitting that he gets called one at the end. That's essentially what *Walker* means—humbug, nonsense. We know it was part of a longer expression, *Hookey Walker*, but that's all we know for sure today. There is an interesting origin story (though no doubt apocryphal) recorded in the 1894 *Dictionary of Phrase and Fable*: Hookey was the nickname of Mr. John Walker—a clerk in a London publishing house with a notable hooked nose and a bad habit for ratting on his coworkers. As everyone always denied everything that Walker said, the name "Hookey Walker" became synonymous with "a tale not to be trusted." That's basically what the incredulous Miss Mowcher says in *David Copperfield*: "Do you know what my great-grandfather's name was¿ . . . It was Walker, my sweet pet . . . and he came of a long line of Walkers, that I inherit all the Hookey estates from."

Yarmouth Bloater

[YAHR-muhth·BLOH-ter] Literally, a whole smoked herring (with *bloat* having an archaic meaning of "to dry by smoke"). It was a popular specialty of the seaside town of Yarmouth, England, and thus applied as a nickname for its residents.

I hinted to Peggotty that . . . if the land had been a little more separated from the sea, and the town and the tide had not been quite so much mixed up, like toast and water, it would have been nicer. But Peggotty said . . . for her part, she was proud to call herself a **Yarmouth Bloater***.*

— DAVID COPPERFIELD

Pinning characters to certain places, and certain social classes, by the way they talked was nothing new to English literature. Writers like Chaucer and Shakespeare had been doing it for centuries. But Dickens did it on a completely unprecedented scale, bigger and better than ever before. Through thousands of pages of dialogue, he recorded, like a literary soundtrack, the vast and varied voices of his Victorian world—from the muddled speech patterns of the poorest servant to the flowery pronunciations of the well-to-do. Capturing London's voices, however, was Dickens' specialty, especially Cockney, a lower-class Victorian dialect originating in East London. For Dickens, Cockney's most distinguishing attribute was its confusing phonetic swaps of v's and w's—something that Sam Weller enthusiastically reminds us in *The Pickwick Papers*, to the endless chagrin of modern readers and modern-day Cockney speakers alike (as the old v/w switch has long since disappeared from their dialect): *"Don't call me Valker; my name's Veller; you know that vell enough."*

"Mostly Prunes and Prism"

WORDS FOR THE RICH
AND RIDICULOUS

Anti-Pickwickian

[AN-tee-pik-WIK-ee-uhn] Ungentlemanly.

---

*Mr. Tracy Tupman . . . had been bestowing sundry **anti-Pickwickian** glances on a young lady by the roadside.*

— THE PICKWICK PAPERS

Truth be told, defining *anti-Pickwickian* is as unrealistic as trying to define the deceptively simple character of Mr. Pickwick himself. Pickwick's exact "meaning" continues to be "sought and hotly debated," wrote one of Dickens' biographers, Percy Fitzgerald, in 1895. And to this day no better word exists to sum up Mr. Pickwick's lovably light-hearted amalgam of kindness, generosity, jollity, and childlike innocence than Dickens' original term "Pickwickian." Even G.K. Chesterton resorted to the abstract when describing this immortal, almost mythical, spirit of English literature:

"Pickwick will always be remembered as the great example of everything that made Dickens great; of the solemn conviviality of great friendships, of the erratic adventures of old English roads, of the hospitality of old English inns, of the great fundamental kindliness and honour of old English manners."

Beadlehood

[BEE-dl-hood] Pomposity over petty authority, a stereotypical trait of Victorian *beadles*—minor officials hired by the Anglican Church to dole out discipline, order, and charity in local parishes.

> *Mr. Bumble . . . was in the full bloom and pride of **beadlehood**; his cocked hat and coat were dazzling in the morning sun; he clutched his cane with the vigorous tenacity of health and power.*
>
> — OLIVER TWIST

A far more popular synonym for beadlehood is *bumbledom*, appropriately named after the beadle who besmirched the name of all beadles forever, Mr. Bumble in *Oliver Twist*. To be fair, Bumble isn't the first bombastic beadle in Dickens' oeuvre. Simmons the beadle appeared years prior, in *Sketches by Boz*, with similar assumptions that he was "one of the most, perhaps *the* most, important member of the local administration." What made Mr. Bumble different was not only his superior name—though superior it is; he's simply a superior practitioner of beadlehood. Yes, he works for a local "charity," surrounded by poverty and starvation, but inconvenient emotions are never allowed to cloud the all-importance of his work. Tears were "tokens of weakness" for Mr. Bumble, whose "heart was . . . rendered stouter" by any suffering around him. Of course, this attitude helps a great deal when starving orphans, like Oliver Twist, waddle up to you asking for a bit more gruel.

Bumptious

[BUMP-shuss] Conceited, likely based on the connotations of swelling and swollenness in the word *bump*. Thus, being *bumptious* is being swollen with conceit.

---

*His hair was very smooth and wavy; but I was informed . . . that it was a wig . . . and that he needn't be so "bounceable"— somebody else said "**bumptious**"—about it, because his own red hair was very plainly to be seen behind.*

— DAVID COPPERFIELD

Dickens was a bit bumptious about his hair too. For one, he obsessively combed his wavy brown locks "a hundred times a day," according to one of his employees. And Dickens never seemed to know when (or when not) to whip out his comb, a fact demonstrated at a dinner party in Boston in 1842 and recorded by Edward F. Payne:

Great mirrors were everywhere in the forties [1840s], and Boz, catching sight of his reflection across the dinner table and not being entirely satisfied with the arrangement of his long and poetic locks, calmly took a pocket comb from his pocket and combed his hair at the table—an act which . . . [was] received with many expressions of amused astonishment.

Circumlocution Office

[sur-kuhm-loh-KYOO-shuhn·AW-fis] Dickens' fictional bastion of bureaucratic confusion and red tape, from the Latin *circumlocutio*, "roundabout speech."

> The **Circumlocution Office** was (as everybody knows without being told) the most important Department under Government. . . . Whatever was required to be done, the Circumlocution Office was beforehand with all the public departments in the art of perceiving— *HOW NOT TO DO IT.*
>
> — LITTLE DORRIT

Dickens was one of the first writers to make the pejorative meaning of "red tape" popular, finding the actual red tape that bound British legal documents to be a perfect metaphor for all of their impossibly tight restrictions. Dickens makes "red tape" references in *Hard Times, David Copperfield,* and, of course, *Little Dorrit,* where the Circumlocution Office produces enough of it "to stretch, in graceful festoons, from Hyde Park Corner to the General Post Office"—about three miles. That doesn't seem like much, given that modern red tape measurements usually stretch to the moon and back, but it's quite enough for Daniel Doyce. Dickens' hapless inventor spends twelve tortuous years in the Circumlocution Office, trying to get his invention patented while wading through an endless paper trail of "form-filling . . . signing, counter-signing, counter-counter-signing backwards and forwards, and referring sideways, crosswise, and zig-zag." Doyce finally abandons the office's ineptitudes altogether and takes his intellectual property to another country. Dickens, truth be told, often felt like doing the same.

Coriolanian

[kor-ee-uh-LAY-nee-uhn] Snobby.

---

*Mrs. Sparsit's **Coriolanian** nose underwent a slight expansion of the nostrils, and her black eyebrows contracted as she took a sip of tea.*

— HARD TIMES

It's an amusing irony that Mrs. Sparsit should boast anything *Coriolanian*. The word is an allusion to Shakespeare's titular character Coriolanus, an aristocratic Roman general who, rather like Mrs. Sparsit herself, has a haughty disdain for the working classes.* But Mrs. Sparsit really needs to get off her high Roman horse. As Mr. Bounderby's housekeeper in *Hard Times*, she's a bona fide member of the same class she scoffs at. Although, of course, Mrs. Sparsit never admits to anything of the sort and stubbornly insists on referring to her yearly salary as an "annual compliment."

*What does a Coriolanian nose look like? Dickens, unsurprisingly, describes it as "Roman"— the Victorian catchword for a nose with a high, prominent bridge (creating a somewhat beak-like appearance that was often termed *aquiline*, from the Latin for "eagle"). Quite the fitting accompaniment to Mrs. Sparsit's "hawk's eyes."

Curl-papers

[kurl-PAY-pers] The nineteenth-century (paper) equivalent of plastic hair curlers.

---

*"Who's there?" screamed a numerous chorus of treble voices from the staircase inside, consisting of the spinster lady of the establishment, three teachers, five female servants, and thirty boarders, all half-dressed and in a forest of **curl-papers**.*

— THE PICKWICK PAPERS

No thrifty Victorian would dream of buying curl-papers. They were, after all, simple and cheap to make—any scrap of paper could be cut up for the purpose. Triangular pieces, a couple of inches wide, were the most common choice. These bits of paper, when twisted around the hair, gave off the iconic head-full-of-paper-butterflies look (the fancy word for curl-paper being papillote, based on the French word for "butterfly"). However, if you were a real snoot and insisted on buying curl-paper, you had to be extra careful to make your meaning clear. Curl-paper was also the nineteenth-century euphemism for toilet paper. Indeed, why anyone would buy either was a complete mystery to most Victorians. Store-bought toilet paper was available in Britain in the late eighteen hundreds, but even that looked (and felt) exactly like what everyone was already using throughout the century. This was the uncomfortable era when toilet paper really meant paper—any scrap paper they might have lying around the house would do. Yes, the same stuff they curled their hair with.

Epergne

[eh-PURN] A large, expensive, and purely ornamental centerpiece of Victorian tables. Somewhat similar to a candelabra, it consisted of extended arms holding elevated dishes, from the French *épargne*, "a saving or treasury."

Everything [on the table] was made to look as heavy as it could, and to take up as much room as possible . . . [especially the] corpulent straddling **epergne***, blotched all over as if it had broken out in an eruption rather than been ornamented.*

— OUR MUTUAL FRIEND

If you had a corpulent epergne on your nineteenth-century dinner table, then jolly congratulations—you had financially arrived. Nothing, after all, screamed wealth and luxury more clearly to Victorians than uselessly large knickknacks. And epergnes screamed it the loudest: "Here you have as much of me in my ugliness as if I were only lead," Dickens could almost hear them boast, "but I am so many ounces of precious metal worth so much an ounce; —wouldn't you like to melt me down?" But be careful how you answer these silvery sirens of status. Wealth and happiness rarely collide in the Dickensian universe: just ask Miss Havisham. She possesses the most famous epergne in all of English literature, though it's certainly not one to gloat over. Grotesquely "overhung with cobwebs" and "black fungus" the epergne is now the home of "speckled-legged spiders"—the consequence of Miss Havisham's table not having been inhabited by a happy human guest for twenty-five years. Dickens' moral? Wealth, if not shared often and well, is as useless as an empty epergne.

Experientia Does It

[ik-SPEER-ee-in-shuh·dohz·it]   Mrs. Micawber's famous misrendering of the Latin maxim, *experientia docet*, "experience teaches."

> *"I never thought,"* said Mrs. Micawber . . . *"before I was married, when I lived with papa and mama, that I should ever find it necessary to take a lodger. . . . I really should have hardly understood what the word meant, in the sense in which I now employ it, but* **experientia does it**, *—as papa used to say."*
>
> — DAVID COPPERFIELD

It isn't surprising that what classical Latin Mrs. Micawber knows (or doesn't) she had to overhear. "Girls never learn such things" as Tom Tulliver tells his sister in George Eliot's *The Mill on the Floss* (1860). And in general, he was right. Education for eighteenth- and nineteenth-century girls was elementary, at best. Higher intellectual pursuits, like learning Latin, Greek, and advanced mathematics, were deemed outside their mental capacity and totally irrelevant to their future duties as wives and mothers. Girls are just "too silly!" as Tom Tulliver bluntly puts it. It's a cringe-worthy thought today, though once reflected in the incredibly silly "schools" for girls that parade through Dickens' fiction. Among their lackluster lot there's Minerva House in *Sketches by Boz* where "young ladies . . . acquired a smattering of everything, and a knowledge of nothing." At Mrs. Wackles "Ladies' Seminary" in *The Old Curiosity Shop*, legitimate courses include "dancing" and "general fascination." The purpose of which? To get a husband, of course, and to begin the whole silly cycle all over again.

Farinagholkajingo

[fuh-REE-nuh-gohl-ka-jing-goh] Dickens' pretentious term for any fashionable, newfangled dance. It's uncertain if Dickens invented *farinagholkajingo*, since it appears in an 1843 article in *Punch* describing a dance that "was always promised" to guests at balls though "which no one ever saw or comprehended."

---

*[This is] my daughter, sir . . . who I hope will have the pleasure of dancing many a quadrille, minuet, gavotte, country-dance, fandango, double-hornpipe, and **farinagholkajingo** with you, sir. She dances them all, sir; and so shall you, sir, before you're a quarter older, sir."*

— SKETCHES BY BOZ

For many Victorians, the social ladder looked more like a shiny ball-room floor: one didn't climb it so much as dance across it. On the one hand, dancing was totally classless, a nineteenth-century amusement for both poor and rich alike. But how you danced, and what dances you knew, demonstrated where you fit into society. And learning to dance well (in emulation of the wealthy) was a priority for the upwardly mobile middle classes. This is why *farinagholkajingo* appears, appropriately, in Dickens' short sketch, "The Dancing Academy," a humorous look into one of the many dance schools scattered throughout Victorian London, many of which ran on the pretentious promise of turning out fashionable gentlemen and ladies after a few twirling lessons. Though, as Dickens points out, the majority of these academies were "decidedly cheap," which obviously indicates that their clients were hardly the rich ladies and gentlemen they so desired to be.

Fortunatus's Purse

[FOR-tyoo-nah-tuhs-iz·purs] An endless supply, in reference to a medieval German fairy tale wherein the hero, Fortunatus, is given a magical purse that continuously replenishes itself with money.

---

*Perhaps there never was a more moral man than Mr. Pecksniff. . . . It was once said of him by a homely admirer, that he had a **Fortunatus's purse** of good sentiments in his inside.*

— MARTIN CHUZZLEWIT

In 1867, three years before his death, Dickens wrote *The Magic Fishbone*, his first and only fairy tale for children. Though it reads a bit sappy today, it was Dickens' sincere attempt to give back to a genre that he felt had given him so much. Through fairy tales, Dickens first fell in love with the concept of hope—hope in the face of bleakness. As a boy, he believed Little Red Riding Hood embodied that vision: "I felt that if I could have married Little Red Riding-Hood, I would have known perfect bliss." As a writer, fairy-tale motifs and happy endings had a persistent habit of creeping into his fiction. Even when Dickens seriously considered ending *Great Expectations* on a tragic note, he was easily convinced to change the last chapter, giving Pip and Estella, if not an actual happy ending, at least the hope of one. It was, he knew deep down, a message his jaded, industrial-age readers desperately needed to be reminded of: "In an utilitarian age, of all other times, it is a matter of grave importance that Fairy Tales should be respected . . . a nation without fancy, without some romance, never did, never can, never will, hold a great place under the sun."

Haggerawators

[hag-UHR-ah-way-ters] Locks of hair twisted into curls and greased to lay down flat on the forehead, near the temple. Also called *aggerawators*, with both words being corruptions of *aggravators*. It's not entirely clear, but *aggravate*, from Latin, literally means "to weigh down," which is exactly what the hair is being coaxed into doing here.

---

*Mr. Samuel Wilkins was a carpenter, a journeyman carpenter of small dimensions; decidedly below the middle size — bordering, perhaps, upon the dwarfish. His face was round and shining and his hair carefully twisted into the outer corner of each eye till it formed a variety of that description of semi-curls, usually known as "**haggerawators**."*

— SKETCHES BY BOZ

Mr. Samuel Wilkins might want to think twice before getting his haggerawators in a twist again. These greasy curls were definitely on their way out of vogue when Dickens wrote those lines in 1836. In fact, haggerawators eventually took on the nickname of "Newgate Knockers," as they bore a comic resemblance to the iron door knockers on the entrance to Newgate Prison in London, and were gaudily sported by many of its residents. Obviously, when inmates start emulating your hairstyle, it's time to get a new one.

Hartshorning

[HAHRTS-hawr-ning] Administering smelling salts.

---

*After a vast amount of moaning and crying up-stairs, and much damping of foreheads, and vinegaring of temples, and **hartshorning** of noses . . . the locksmith humbled himself, and the end was gained.*

— BARNABY RUDGE

If nineteenth-century novels are to be believed, fainting spells afflicted English ladies on an epidemic scale. Their one reliable recourse? Smelling salts. Essentially a vial of ammonia, the smelling salt bottle had only to be waved under the nose of the afflicted swooner for its powerful vapors to get to work, irritating the nasal passage and triggering a reactionary (and reviving) gasp for breath. Also known as "spirits of hartshorn," from the historic practice of obtaining ammonia from the antlers (or *horns*) of deers (*hart* being an archaic word for "stag"), smelling salts were among the strongest substances in the Victorian health arsenal. Mr. Bounderby in *Hard Times* figures as much when he purchases a bottle from a local chemist: "'By George!' said Mr. Bounderby, 'if she takes it in the fainting way, I'll have the skin off her nose, at all events!'"

Honorificabilitudinitatibus

[ON-uh-rif-i-KAH-bi-li-TOO-din-i-ta-ti-buhs] A purposefully pretentious, Latinized rendering of "honorableness." Dickens uses it in the following quote to poke fun at science's obsession with long, difficult words.

---

*He who by the seashore makes friends with the sea-nettles, is introduced to them by the scientific master of ceremonies as the Physsophoridae and Hippopodydae. Creatures weak, delicate and beautiful, are Desmidiaceae, Chaetopterina, and Amphino-maceae, Tenthredineta, Twentysyllableorfeeta, and all for the honour of science; or rather, not for its honour; but for it **honorificabilitudinitatibus**.*

— HOUSEHOLD WORDS

Honorificabilitudinitatibus got its first chuckle from Shakespeare, who famously used it in his comedy *Love's Labour's Lost* (in similar mockery of pretentious and long-winded language). Of course this is where Dickens got the word and idea from, and where so much of his inspiration ultimately sprang. Simply put, Dickens turned to Shakespeare as "the great master who knew everything." Everything, that is, about constructing the perfect comic and tragic scenes—as Nicholas Nickleby says, about turning "familiar things into constellations which should enlighten the world for ages," everything that Dickens himself spent a lifetime pursuing. Many are convinced that Dickens came closer to anyone in that pursuit: among them, literary critic F.R. Leavis emphasized Dicken's powerful "command of word, phrase, rhyme, and image: in ease and range there is surely no greater master of English except Shakespeare."

Infant Phenomenon

[IN-fuhnt·fi-NOM-uh-non] A generic stage name for child actors in the nineteenth century: the Victorian equivalent of "child star," with *infant* being used in its more general meaning of "child," not newborn.

"My daughter—my daughter," replied Mr. Vincent Crummles; "the idol of every place we go into, sir" . . . Mr. Crummles stopped: language was not powerful enough to describe the **infant phenomenon**.

— NICHOLAS NICKLEBY

Cue spotlight on Miss Ninetta Crummles, the curly-haired child wonder of the Crummles company of traveling actors—just the sort of "natural genius" that could go on to teach Shirley Temple everything she knows. At least that's how her proud parents feel about it. The rest of the company isn't too sure. Ninetta never utters a single word, and her only perceivable talent appears to be giddily twirling about on stage. "Infant humbug," whispers fellow actor Mr. Folair. There's also a rumor circulating that she's not even a child. Hmm, possibly because she's been advertised as being ten years old for the past five years? Either that or her "unlimited allowance of gin-and-water" has permanently stunted her growth. The real-life rumor is that Dickens modeled Ninetta on the actual Victorian child star Jean Davenport. Billed by her very Crummles-like family as "the most celebrated juvenile actress of the day," Davenport began her long career on the stage at age eight and was, by all accounts, a very talented actress—though how many "infant phenomenon" jokes the poor woman had to endure thanks to Dickens is inconceivable.

L.S.D.-ically

[el-es-dee-i-kuh-lee] Monetarily. L.S.D. is the phonetic rendering of £sd—Britain's pre-decimal currency system composed of pounds, shillings, and pence, originally applying to Roman coin and weight measurements: *librae*, *solidi*, and *denarii*.

> *[The Major's hard work] is a thing that ought to be known to the Throne and Lords and Commons and then might [we] obtain some promotion for the Major which he well deserves and would be none the worse for (speaking between friends)* **L.S.D.-ically.**
>
> — MRS. LIRRIPER'S LODGINGS

Brace yourself: We're about to plunge into the bewildering world of Victorian money as Dickens knew it. Let's start with the easy bit. A pound equals 20 shillings, a shilling equals 12 pence, and it takes 240 pence to bring us back to a pound. Got that? Good. Now enter the coins and the confusion. A *guinea* is worth 21 shillings (just to make things difficult). A *sovereign* is an even pound (20 shillings), and five shillings makes a *crown*. There was also a *florin* piece (2 shillings) and a panoply of penny coins like *groats* (fourpence), threepence, twopence, and a farthing, equaling ¼ pence (because who really wants to break a penny?). And don't forget about the variety of Victorian slang terms for money, the more popular being *quid*, for a pound, and *bob*, for a shilling. Ring a bell? Bob Cratchit, in *A Christmas Carol*, makes "but fifteen 'Bob' a-week himself."

Mercuries

[MUR-kyuh-reez] The Victorian nickname for *footmen*—high-ranking male servants in wealthy households—originally prized for their speed and swiftness, just like the Roman god Mercury (the one with the wings on his sandals).

It is morning in the great world; afternoon according to the little sun. The **Mercuries**, *exhausted by looking out of window, are reposing in the hall; and hang their heavy heads, the gorgeous creatures, like overblown sunflowers.*

— BLEAK HOUSE

Dickens' Mercuries look pretty immobile—not exactly like swift Roman gods and certainly not like their historic predecessors. In centuries prior, footmen really knew what it was to use their feet. Once known as "running footmen," they were employed to run ahead of their master's carriage, removing obstacles from bumpy roads and preparing for their arrival at journey's end. An indispensable luxury throughout the seventeenth and eighteenth centuries, the practice of dispatching Mercuries had almost entirely disappeared by Dickens' day. But footmen remained. Retaining their luxury status, they gradually moved indoors and became practically ornamental, literally paid to stand tall and project as much wealth as possible. Tall, handsome footmen were in highest demand (note how Dickens calls them "gorgeous creatures"). Granted, footmen did have their various duties: mostly serving at table, answering the door, running errands, and delivering messages. The latter job might have contributed to footmen still being called Mercuries in the nineteenth century—in mythology, Mercury was also the messenger of the gods.

Nobby

[**NOB**-ee] Stylish. British aristocrats were once known as *nobs*, a contraction of "nobles" or "nobility."

> It must not be supposed that our watering-place is an empty place, deserted by all visitors. . . . So far from being at a discount as to company, we are in fact what would be popularly called rather a **nobby** place. Some tip-top "Nobbs" come down occasionally—even Dukes and Duchesses.
>
> — OUR ENGLISH WATERING-PLACE

The nobby place Dickens is describing is Broadstairs—a seaside town on the southeast coast of England. Beginning in 1837, Dickens and his family spent many late-summer holidays at Broadstairs, recharging in its "intensely quiet" surroundings of "good sea—fresh breezes—fine sands—and pleasant walks." At first Dickens cheerily reported that "Nobody bothers him" at Broadstairs and he was able to write in quiet seclusion with only the sound of the "sea rolling and dashing under" his study windows. But by 1847 Broadstairs was becoming altogether too nobby (and noisy) for Dickens' liking: "Vagrant music is getting to that height here, and is so impossible to be escaped from, that I fear Broadstairs and I must part company in time to come."

Physiognomist

[fiz-ee-OG-nuh-mist] A person who judges moral character based solely on facial characteristics, from the Greek *phusis*, "nature," and *gnomon*, "a judge."

> *The landlord, whether he was a good or a bad **physiognomist**, had fully made up his mind that the guest was an ill-looking fellow.*
>
> — LITTLE DORRIT

Dating back to the early Greeks and mentioned by Shakespeare, the spurious "science" of physiognomy found a captivated audience in the Victorians*—a group notoriously quick to judge books by their covers. Dickens himself owned a treatise on the subject and constantly created literary characters under physiognomy's basic premise—that goodness bears a beautiful face, evil an ugly one. In *Oliver Twist* Dickens played the amateur physiognomist more directly when he has Mr. Brownlow confront the evil—and thus, unattractive—Monks: "you . . . in whom all evil passions, vice, and profligacy, festered, till they found a vent in a hideous disease which has made your face an index even to your mind."

*Its legacy continues in modern-day Britain, where popular slangs for a person's face (*phiz*, *phizog*, *fizzog*, etc.) all derive from physiognomy and the historic trouble of pronouncing it.

Plenipotentiary

[plen-uh-puh-TEN-shee-er-ee] A person invested with full powers, usually on behalf of a government, from the Latin *plenus*, "full," and *potentia*, "power."

---

*This led to Mr. Wopsle's (who had never been heard of before) coming in with a star and garter on, as a **plenipotentiary** of great power direct from the Admiralty.*

— GREAT EXPECTATIONS

Dickens' celebrity status opened a few plenipotentiary doors in his day. He was received at the White House and met two American presidents, though he was rather unimpressed with his "conference" with President John Tyler in 1842, finding him somewhat dull and "so jaded." Brazenly, Dickens snubbed Tyler's invitation to a White House dinner a few days later. He was never one to fawn over persons of power. Dickens did, however, become a bit weak in the knees in 1870 when he was summoned to Buckingham Palace for a private audience with Queen Victoria. By all accounts, it was an awkward meeting. They talked briefly of Dickens' travels and (rather oddly) of the current price of food and the availability of good servants. The Queen ended the interview by presenting Dickens with a copy of her recently written book, *Leaves from the Journal of Our Life in the Highlands*. Dickens accepted the gift with the utmost grace, no doubt suppressing his earlier opinion of the Queen's published work as a "preposterous book."

Podsnappery

[pod-SNAP-er-ee] Self-satisfied smugness and a willful disinterest in the affairs and opinions of others, the eponymous personality of Mr. Podsnap in *Our Mutual Friend*.

It was a trait in Mr. Podsnap's character (and in one form or other it will be generally seen to pervade the depths and shallows of **Podsnappery**), *that he could not endure a hint of disparagement of any friend or acquaintance of his. "How dare you¿" he would seem to say, in such a case. . . . "Through this person you strike at me, Podsnap the Great."*

— OUR MUTUAL FRIEND

Before charging anyone with the crimes of Podsnappery, it's best to become acquainted with Dickens' original offender:

Mr. Podsnap was well to do, and stood very high in Mr. Podsnap's opinion . . . and was quite satisfied. He never could make out why everybody was not quite satisfied, and he felt conscious that he set a brilliant social example in being particularly well satisfied with most things, and, above all other things, with himself. Thus happily acquainted with his own merit and importance, Mr. Podsnap settled that whatever he put behind him he put out of existence. There was a dignified conclusiveness—not to add a grand convenience—in this way of getting rid of disagreeables . . . Mr. Podsnap had even acquired a peculiar flourish of his right arm in often clearing the world of its most difficult problems, by sweeping them behind him (and consequently sheer away).

Prunes and Prism

[proonz·and·PRIZ-uhm] Dickens' shorthand for ladylike politeness. Part of a phonetic exercise, the words "prunes and prism" would theoretically form the mouth into a demure and attractive shape.

---

*Little Dorrit, still habitually thoughtful and solitary, though no longer alone, at first supposed this [polite conversation] to be mere **Prunes and Prism**.*

— LITTLE DORRIT

Literature had its first taste of *prunes and prism* in the introductory diatribe of Mrs. General, Little Dorrit's tyrannical chaperone hired to "polish" and "varnish" her for elegant society. They appear in her ridiculously memorable list of words that give "a pretty form to the lips": "Papa, potatoes, poultry, prunes, and prism, are all very good words for the lips: especially prunes and prism." Especially indeed, as Dickens went on to use "prunes and prism" seventeen times in *Little Dorrit*. He knew he had stumbled upon the perfect catchphrase for the restricted Victorian woman: forced to meet the world with pursed lips (physically and figuratively), in an endless parade of meaningless manners. It was a brilliant metaphor and was soon on the decrying tongues of literature's female rebels, most memorably Jo from *Little Women*: "If I was a boy, we'd run away together, and have a capital time, but as I'm a miserable girl, I must be proper and stop at home . . . 'Prunes and prisms' are my doom."

Pumblechookian

[puhm-buhl-CHOO-kee-uhn] Typical of Mr. Pumblechook, Pip's pompous, greedy, and hypocritical uncle in *Great Expectations*.

---

*Mr. Wopsle had in his hand the affecting tragedy of George Barnwell . . . with the view of heaping every word of it on the head of Pumblechook, with whom he was going to drink tea. No sooner did he see me, than he appeared to consider that a special Providence had put a 'prentice in his way to be read at; and he . . . insisted on my accompanying him to the **Pumblechookian** parlour.*

— GREAT EXPECTATIONS

Deciphering Dickensian character names is a tricky business. Thankfully, Mr. Pumblechook is a fairly easy exception to that rule. The *chook* in Pumblechook is evidently a quirky replacement for "choke." After all, he's first introduced in the novel as a "hard-breathing" man who looks "as if he had just been all but choked." Choking, usually equated with overeating, is Dickens' initial tip-off that Pumblechook's character is primed for greed and gluttony. Endlessly infuriating, he's also primed for a punch or two, which brings us to the *pumble* in Pumblechook. *Pumble* was an early variant of *pummel*, "to beat or hit repeatedly," or as Pip himself admits: "I used to want . . . to burst into spiteful tears, fly at Pumblechook, and pummel him all over."

Quizzing-glass

[KWIZ-ing-glas] A small, handheld magnifying lens—a monocle, as it were, with a handle—from the archaic verb *quiz*, meaning "to look closely and inquisitively at something."

---

*[Mr. Micawber] carried a jaunty sort of a stick, with a large pair of rusty tassels to it; and a **quizzing-glass** hung outside his coat,—for ornament, I afterwards found, as he very seldom looked through it, and couldn't see anything when he did.*

— DAVID COPPERFIELD

This ornamental quizzing-glass is our first indicator that Mr. Micawber is a bit of a *dandy*—the Victorian equivalent of a metrosexual—and the sort of person Dickens' friend Thomas Carlyle would have called "a clothes-wearing man." Carlyle explains further: "A dandy is . . . a man whose trade, office, and existence consists in the wearing of clothes. Every faculty of his soul, spirit, purse, and person is heroically consecrated to this one object, the wearing of clothes wisely and well." Sartorially speaking, this sums up Mr. Micawber pretty well: his clothes, though shabby, are always worn with "imposing" style.

Rattle-pated

[RAT'l-pat-id] Lacking sense or focus, with *pate* being an archaic term for "head"—a head containing so few brains, it "rattles" more than it thinks.

> *He was one of those reckless, **rattle-pated**, open-hearted, and open-mouthed young gentlemen, who possess the gift of familiarity in its highest perfection, and who scramble carelessly along the journey of life making friends, as the phrase is, wherever they go.*
>
> — THE LAZY TOUR OF TWO IDLE APPRENTICES

This passage could easily be describing any of Dickens' own sons—seven of them—who constantly failed to live up to their father's ambitiously high standards. And Dickens had no qualms with pronouncing his frustrated verdict on each one. His firstborn, Charley, had "less fixed purpose and energy than I could have supposed possible in my son." Next came Walter, who "spends more than he gets and has cost me money and disappointed me." Then there was Frank who, frankly, was "not at all brilliant," and Sydney, who had "an inveterate habit of drawing bills, that will ruin him." The youngest, Plorn (born Edward), was constantly in "want of application and continuity of purpose." For the most part, Alfred and Henry escaped these sad assessments, eventually living lives, as Dickens saw, filled with a "wholesome sense of responsibility." As for the rest, Dickens lamented to a friend two years before his death: "Why was I ever a father!"

Reticule

[RET-i-kyool] A small pouch-shaped purse (with a strap)—the predecessor to the modern woman's handbag.

"Your uncle has taken a strong fancy to you, that's quite clear; and if some extraordinary good fortune doesn't come to you, after this, I shall be a little surprised, that's all." With this she launched out into sundry anecdotes of young ladies, who had had thousand-pound notes given them in **reticules**, *by eccentric uncles.*

— NICHOLAS NICKLEBY

Reticules came in two general styles. The first was a floppy little sack of fabric tied with a drawstring on top. It looked rather like a drawn-up net when fastened (hence, why reticule comes from the Latin *reticulum*, "little net"). The second style was floppy like the first, though it was secured with a metal clasp on top. This is the sort of reticule Miss Murdstone prefers in *David Copperfield*, as she enjoys the way the metal clasp closes "up like a bite" (rather like her lips, we are told). Either way, reticules were all inconveniently small—a tiny clutch-style handbag would be its closest modern equivalent. In 1801, the diarist Katherine Wilmot claimed that a lady could stuff a snuffbox, handkerchief, fan, coin purse, love letter, prayer book, visiting cards, and candy in hers. But that was stretching it (the fabric) enormously. For incommodious reasons like that, reticules became known as *ridicules* almost instantly—that simple two-letter exchange being all too irresistible, especially for Dickens. In *Oliver Twist*, he lists "women's ridicules" as one of the easiest things to rob.

Sabbatarian

[sab-uh-TAIR-ee-uhn] A nineteenth-century supporter of strict laws enforcing Sunday as a day of rest.

---

*Manage the proofs . . . so that I may not have to correct them on a Sunday. I am not going over to the **Sabbatarians**, but like the haystack (particularly) on a Sunday morning.*

— LETTERS OF CHARLES DICKENS

The "Observance question"—or how should one properly observe the Christian Sabbath day—was a hot-button issue for Victorian society. On one side of the ecclesiastic aisle, Dickens believed that Sunday was a sacred time for innocent "amusements and recreations," especially for the poor (who toiled under a six-day workweek at the time). On the other side, characters such as Mr. Gallanbile in *Nicholas Nickleby* advocated for sterner observances of Sabbath laws, petitioning Parliament to shut down all pubs, theaters, museums, and retail shops on Sunday. Of course, wealthy Mr. Gallanbile has to humorously and hypocritically circumvent the fact that his own servants still have to work on Sunday; a double standard Dickens is quick to satirize:

Mr. Gallanbile being devoted to the Observance question [insists that] . . . No victuals whatever [are] cooked on the Lord's Day, with the exception of dinner for Mr. and Mrs. Gallanbile, which, being a work of piety and necessity, is exempted.

Spatterdashes

[SPAT-er-dash-iz] Knee-high leg coverings (usually made of leather) for keeping trousers clean on horseback, so called because they "dashed away" spatters of mud.

---

*Although he seemed, judging from the mud he had picked up on the way, to have come from London, his horse was as smooth and cool as his own iron-grey periwig and pigtail. Neither man nor beast had turned a single hair . . . saving for his soiled skirts and **spatterdashes**.*

— BARNABY RUDGE

As England's roads improved during the late nineteenth century,* so too did spatterdashes—though their improvements were entirely ornamental. Victorian fashionistas shortened their name to "spats" and cut off most of their height as well. These posher ankle-high coverings (usually white) became a must-have for the respectably dressed gentlemen about town—a style that persisted into the 1920s (on both sides of the Atlantic), as referenced in Irving Berlin's iconic song of fashionable wealth, "Puttin' on the Ritz": "Have you seen the well-to-do, up and down Park Avenue . . . High hats and arrow collars, white spats and lots of dollars."

*Prior to this improvement, the muddy, dusty state of England's roads can be surmised from *David Copperfield*. When David walks from London to Dover, he arrives at his aunt's house "From heat to foot . . . powdered almost . . . white with chalk and dust."

Spoffish

[SPOF-ish] Bustling and active, especially in a trivial way, from the English dialect verb *spoffle*, "to look busily engaged over matters of little importance."

---

*He was always making something for somebody, or planning some party of pleasure, which was his great forte. He invariably spoke with astonishing rapidity; was smart, **spoffish**, and eight-and-twenty.*

— SKETCHES BY BOZ

If you'd like to learn the art of looking busy without actually doing any work, Dickens offers some top-notch examples. His best take the occupational form of barristers—Victorian lawyers with notorious reputations for laziness. In *The Pickwick Papers*, a group of them loiter about a courtroom, carrying trivial legal documents "in as conspicuous a manner as possible . . . to impress the fact more strongly" that they were hard at work. In *Our Mutual Friend*, Eugene Wrayburn (another idle barrister) even walks in a spoffish manner: "lazily," but still actively "holding possession of twice as much pavement as another would have claimed." Yet barristers do get somewhat of a reprieve in *A Tale of Two Cities*. The character Sydney Carton might be a do-nothing barrister at the start of the story, but he ends up a hero through an act of selfless sacrifice, giving fresh irony to his famous last thought: "It is a far, far better thing I do, than I have ever done . . . "

The Peerage

[thuh·PEER-ij] A reference to one of the many *peerage* guides, annual publications detailing the genealogies and residences of Britain's aristocratic families, the most popular being *Burke's Peerage* and *Debrett's Peerage*.

---

*He knew the **peerage** by heart, and, could tell you, off-hand, where any illustrious personage lived.*

— SKETCHES BY BOZ

You might think of peerage guides as wonderfully detailed phone books for the rich and fabulous. Everyone of rank could be found in the Peerage pages, along with their family history and lists of presumptive heirs. For snobs, like Oscar Wilde's Lord Illingworth, they were "the best thing in fiction the English have ever done." For social climbers, peerage guides were invaluable teaching tools, breaking down the British aristocratic system for every confused commoner and instructing them on how to address the vast and varied world of their betters. Starting at the top were the nation's "peers." These, in descending order of precedence, were dukes, marquesses, earls, viscounts, and barons. A duke was addressed as "Your Grace," a marquess, earl, or viscount as "My Lord," and a baron would be appeased with just "Lord So-and-So." Below the peers were the baronets and knights—both addressed with a simple "Sir" in front of their names. The "Sir" implies the title, something that Mr. Bucket in *Bleak House* could never understand. He always insists on calling the head of the Dedlock family "Sir Leicester Dedlock, Baronet"—a totally redundant addition, as every snob would know.

Tom Tiddler's Ground

[tom·tid·lers·ground] A place where money is easily made. Tom Tiddler's ground was a popular children's game in which, in some versions, one player guards a pile of stones (serving as imaginary pieces of gold and silver) that other players attempt to steal without getting caught.

Now, the spacious dining-room, with the company seated round the glittering table, busy with their glittering spoons, and knives and forks, and plates, might have been taken for a grown-up exposition of **Tom Tiddler's ground***, where children pick up gold and silver.*

— DOMBEY AND SON

Victorian dinner parties were the power lunches of their day. Just look at who's invited to Mr. Dombey's glittering meal—or should we say business meeting? There are "chairmen of public companies", an affluent banker, "reputed to be able to buy up anything," and a fabulously rich old woman "stuffed with bank-notes." No wonder this party is put on specifically for the "cultivation of society," by which Dickens means the cultivation of wealth. Notice the agriculture analogy. Parties like these were incredibly fertile grounds (Tom Tiddler's grounds) of wealth, ripe with opportunities for creating more of it. And for those willing to do some professional smooching, business deals could be struck, life-changing loans granted, and valuable investment advice procured—all before dessert. Just be careful. When Betsey Trotwood in *David Copperfield* invests in some "Tom Tidler nonsense," it ends up financially ruining her. Every game has its losers.

Trumpery

[TRUHM-puh-ree] Something of apparent value, but of little actual worth. From Middle French *tromper*, "to deceive."

---

*And what a man Mr. Chuzzlewit was, sir! Ah! what a man he was. You may talk of your lord mayors . . . your sheriffs, your common councilmen, your **trumpery**; but show me a man in this city who is worthy to walk in the shoes of the departed Mr. Chuzzlewit.*

— MARTIN CHUZZLEWIT

You wouldn't guess it from the above passage, but the celebrated name of Chuzzlewit was an awful conundrum for Dickens. He had contracted himself in 1841 to write a new novel, but couldn't seem to figure out what its titular hero would be called. He tried out several surnames: Sweezleden, Sweezleback, Sweezlewag, Chuzzletoe, Chuzzleboy, and Chuzzlewig, but couldn't start writing the novel in earnest until he finally settled on Chuzzlewit. While it's a frustrating example, this was the modus operandi for Dickens: his creative juices simply didn't seem to flow until the right title was struck for each novel. *Bleak House* went through a dozen draft titles: among the rejected were "The East Wind," "The Ruined House," and "Tom-all-Alone's." *David Copperfield* evolved from Thomas Mags to David Trotfiled, Trotbury, Copperboy, and Copperstone, while *Little Dorrit* had a prolonged incubation under the fairly good title of "Nobody's Fault." Good, but just not right. Thankfully, Dickens felt the same.

Tuft-hunting

[TUHFT-huhn-ting] Seeking out important people for personal gain. The term originated in English universities where aristocrats wore special tassels (known as *tufts*) on their caps, hence "tuft-hunters" were those who shamelessly sucked up to them.

> *I am hourly strengthened in my old belief that our political aristocracy and our **tuft-hunting** are the death of England.*
>
> — LETTERS OF CHARLES DICKENS

A self-made man, Dickens' animosity toward tuft-hunters is understandable. Born into the lower middle classes, he gained admittance into the highest levels of English society purely by "the sweat of his brow." And without the sin of tuft-hunting himself, Dickens threw literary stones at sycophants whenever possible (which he does, in fact, in every one of his novels). But some stones hit too close to home, and none more notoriously than in the pages of *Bleak House*. The character of Harold Skimpole (his harmless traits in particular) was closely modeled on Dickens' much admired acquaintance and fellow journalist Leigh Hunt. The only problem was that Skimpole has a sinister side: he's a scheming social leech who wins the tuft-hunting lottery, finding full financial support in his rich and generous friend John Jarndyce. Leigh Hunt was justifiably mortified when *Bleak House* was published, and Dickens was quick to apologize. Too little too late. Skimpole was already immortalized in literature, and we've been throwing stones at him ever since.

Uxorious

[uhk-SOHR-ee-uhs] Excessively devoted or submissive to one's wife, from the Latin *uxor*, "wife."

---

*Mr. Watkins Tottle was a rather uncommon compound of strong **uxorious** inclinations, and an unparalleled degree of anti-connubial timidity . . . the idea of matrimony had never ceased to haunt him.*

— SKETCHES BY BOZ

Meek Mr. Tottle and his uxorious brethren were the ridicule of the Victorian world, a society that dogmatically placed husbands and fathers at the pinnacle of the family pyramid. "It is quite possible you may have more talent [than your husband]," read a popular advice book to nineteenth-century wives,* "but this has nothing whatever to do with your position as a woman, which is, and must be, inferior to his as a man." Caught between these societal expectations and sincere love, Dickens carefully laid down the laws of this hierarchy before entering into his own marriage to Catherine Hogarth in 1836. After a brief episode during their engagement where Catherine exerted more feminism than was fitting for the time, Dickens was quick and blunt in his ultimatum: Although he is "warmly and deeply attached" to her, he will offer "no second warning" if her "sullen and inflexible obstinacy" continues. Gulp.

The Wives of England by Sarah Stickney Ellis, 1843.

Valetudinarian

[val-i-too-di-NAIR-ee-uhn] A person who anxiously tries to maintain good health and never get sick, from the Latin, curiously enough, for "sickly."

> *Mrs. Tibbs devoted all her energies to prepare for the reception of the **valetudinarian**. The second-floor front was scrubbed, and washed, and flannelled, till the wet went through to the drawing-room ceiling. Clean white counterpanes, and curtains, and napkins, [and] water-bottles as clear as crystal . . . added to the splendour, and increased the comfort, of the apartment.*
>
> **— SKETCHES BY BOZ**

Mrs. Tibbs offers excellent insight into why good health and clean houses were so inexorably linked in the Victorian mind. Without a solid grasp on germ theory she would have assumed that air was the mysterious conduit of all disease. And Mrs. Tibbs, like all vigilant housekeepers of her day, was on the front line of this airborne battle, making sure that anything that had come in contact with air (i.e., everything in the house) was vigorously and routinely cleaned. It was an endless and backbreaking fight, provoking Mrs. Gargery in *Great Expectations* to consider "cleanliness more uncomfortable and unacceptable than dirt itself." But lucky for her, hard housework was said to come with a bucket-load of residual moral benefits (this being, after all, the age when cleanliness was next to godliness). Quite a man of his time in this regard, Dickens makes the moral/health link as well, lumping together "comfort, cleanliness, and decency" in *Martin Chuzzlewit*.

Wat Tylerish

[waht·TAHY-ler-ish] Socially rebellious, especially of the higher classes.

Sir Leicester has a misgiving that there may be a hidden **Wat Tylerish** *meaning in this expression, and fumes a little.*

— BLEAK HOUSE

The name Wat Tyler would have made any nobleman fume. A humble blacksmith in 1381, Wat Tyler led one of the largest social insurrections in British history and came dangerously close to toppling its hierarchal system. Mustering an army of thousands of peasant rebels, Wat Tyler marched on London and sparred, face to face, with King Richard II before being killed by a loyal subject of the monarch. Five centuries later, Wat Tyler's ghost continued to haunt English aristocrats who, like Sir Leicester Dedlock, had a vested interest in never again resurrecting his memory. But Dickens, having a touch of the political rebel in him, naturally saw matters differently. Writing in *A Child's History of England*, he deemed it "probable" that Wat Tyler "was a man of a much higher nature and a much braver spirit than any of the parasites who exulted then, or have exulted since, over his defeat." Needless to say, *A Child's History of England* was hardly admissible reading in most aristocratic nurseries.

Wiglomeration

[wig-loh-muh-RAY-shuhn] Legal bureaucracy—coined by Dickens, from the archetypal wigs worn by British legal professionals.

> *"More **Wiglomeration**," said he. "It's the only name I know for the thing . . . the whole thing will be vastly ceremonious, wordy, unsatisfactory, and expensive, and I call it, in general, Wiglomeration."*
>
> — BLEAK HOUSE

Like the hapless victims of *Jarndyce v. Jarndyce*, the fictional fiasco of a Chancery case* in *Bleak House*, Dickens had his own dealings with the maddening wiglomeration of England's nineteenth-century legal system. At age thirty-two, he found himself embroiled in a lawsuit against a pirate, plagiarizing publisher. Though settled in Dickens' favor, the publisher immediately declared bankruptcy and Dickens was forced to pay the exorbitant court fees. Fuming from the experience, he vented to a friend: "it is better to suffer a great wrong than to have recourse to the much greater wrong of the law."

---

*Chancery was, in theory, England's court of "equity" or fairness. Unlike the courts of common law (bogged down by rigid rules of precedence), Chancery was created to be far more flexible in doling out justice. Ruled by the Lord Chancellor (who gave the court its name and who could originally pass quick judgments based solely on his discretion), Chancery ironically became all that it was created not to be: bureaucratic, expensive, and painfully slow. Its "one great principal," said Dickens, "is to make business for itself."

Woolsack

[WOOL-sak] A seat of judicial power—an actual, wool-stuffed cushion in Parliament's House of Lords was the seat of the Lord Chancellor, once the chief judge in Britain.

---

*I quite believe that Mr. Micawber saw himself, in his judicial mind's eye, on the **woolsack**.*

— DAVID COPPERFIELD

The woolsack was the hallowed throne of the British legal profession, the place where all of its aspirants wanted to ultimately place their ambitious bums. In *Great Expectations*, mounting "to the woolsack" was one of the professional dreams of Matthew Pocket and, if circumstances had been different, Dickens may well have ended up there himself. At fifteen, Dickens began an apprenticeship at a law firm in London with, no doubt, the hazy future hope of becoming a lawyer, a judge, and—who knows?—even Lord Chancellor one day. Though lucky for his future readers, Dickens made little progress in the legal realm, quitting after two years. "I didn't much like it," he later admitted, it was "a very little world, and a very dull one." It was a fortuitous decision, not only in paving the way for his later entrance as a writer but also in preventing him from entering into a profession he would later despise: "lawgivers are nearly always the obstructers of society, instead of its helpers."

"A Most Anomalous Conjunction of Words"

VOCABULARY FOR THE
SMART-SOUNDING VICTORIAN

All a Taunto

[awl·a·TAWN-toh] Everything in order, having the old nautical meaning of a sailing vessel that is fully rigged and ready for sea, from *autaunt*, Middle French for "as much" or "as much as possible."

---

*"The dear old Crippler!" said Mrs. Badger, shaking her head. "She was a noble vessel. Trim, ship-shape, **all a taunto**, as Captain Swosser used to say. You must excuse me if I occasionally introduce a nautical expression; I was quite a sailor once.*

— BLEAK HOUSE

Dickens was never a sailor, but he did develop a profound appreciation for the sort of tall-masted sailing ships Mrs. Badger is lauding—an appreciation that crystallized on his first trip to America in the winter of 1842. Opting for a speedy ocean crossing, Dickens and his wife boarded the *Britannia*, a modern, yet rickety, wooden paddle steamer that promised to make the crossing in two weeks. It ended up taking eighteen miserable days. The seas and storms were so bad, the steamer's smokestack nearly came crashing down, setting the entire deck on fire and prompting Dickens to write: "what the agitation of a steam-vessel is, on a bad winter's night in the wild Atlantic, it is impossible for the most vivid imagination to conceive." Older and wiser, Dickens returned to England on a slower, though far more steady, sailing vessel, vowing to never "trust myself upon the wide ocean, if it please Heaven, in a steamer again."

Allonging and Mashonging

[uh-LON-ging·and·ma-SHON-ging] The patriotic spirit of France; a botched anglicized rendering of the popular lines of the "Marseillaise," the French national anthem: *Allons* enfant de la Patrie . . . *Marchons, marchons!*

---

*As to Marseilles, we know what Marseilles is [said Mr. Meagles]. It sent the most insurrectionary tune into the world that was ever composed. It couldn't exist without **allonging and marshonging** to something or other—victory or death, or blazes, or something.*

— LITTLE DORRIT

Inconveniently detained at the port of Marseilles (on his return trip to England), Mr. Meagles is in no mood to sing the praises of France. Neither was Dickens, at first. On arriving in Paris in 1846, he found the city "a wicked and detestable place," but was quick to add, paradoxically, "though wonderfully attractive." Months later, that fledgling attraction turned into full-blown "marshonging," as Dickens personally discovered how highly the French people valued art and literature. This quickly placed them, in his artistic mind, as "the first people in the universe." A staunch Francophile from then on, Dickens embarked on a serious study of French and by 1855 was totally fluent in what he gushingly termed, "the celestial language"—an odd, and somehow sacrilegious, statement from the man who would become an English national treasure.

Antediluvian

[an-tee-di-LOO-vee-uhn] Extremely old, almost ridiculously so; coined in the seventeeth-century from a Latin construction essentially meaning "belonging to a time before the Biblical Flood."

---

*That gentleman took from his hat what seemed to be the fossil remains of an **antediluvian** pocket-handkerchief, and wiped his eyes therewith.*

— MARTIN CHUZZLEWIT

Dickens wasn't a big fan of the Old Testament, finding "certain passages" too "sternly, fiercely, wrathfully" written. The fantastic story of Noah's Ark, however, was his personal exception. It had a fairy-tale appeal to Dickens, encompassing a message dear to his heart: one of safety and security from the raging waves of life and a promise of new beginnings. Consequently, a whole armada of ark references sail through many of his novels, most charmingly in *David Copperfield*. The snug ark-like home of Mr. Peggotty, shored "high and dry" on the sands of Yarmouth's coast, is a haven of peace for young David. Little more than a recycled barge with a chimney on top, "it seemed to [David] the most delicious retreat that the imagination of man could conceive. To hear the wind getting up out at sea . . . and think that there was no house near but this one, and this one a boat, was like enchantment."

Articulator

[ahr-TIK-yuh-lay-ter] Someone who separates and/or joins together, from the Latin root *articulus*, "joint."

Silas receives [a business card] . . . which Venus takes from a wonderful litter in a drawer, and putting on his spectacles, reads: "Mr. Venus . . . Preserver of Animals and Birds . . . **Articulator** *of human bones."*

— OUR MUTUAL FRIEND

Mr. Venus' profession as an articulator usually stumps modern readers, who are hardly helped in their understanding by his mysterious shop of horrors where "the general panoramic view" is of nothing but boxes upon boxes of rattling bones. But strip away the morbid Victorian melodrama and Mr. Venus, in current terms, is simply a skeletal reconstructor (a man you might find working in a history museum today, patiently wiring together the bones of a disjointed *Tyrannosaurus rex*). His talent, he tells a customer, is astonishing: "if you was brought here loose in a bag to be articulated, I'd name your smallest bones blindfold equally with your largest, as fast as I could pick 'em out, and I'd sort 'em all . . . in a manner that would equally surprise and charm you." This exquisitely rude remark (given that the customer is still alive) is only excusable due to Mr. Venus' iconic bouts of depression. Surrounded by skeletons all day, he can't help but see everything in a "boney light."

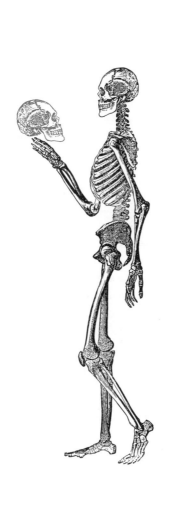

Bedight

[bih-DAHYT] Adorned, with *dight* being an archaic English verb having various meanings of "to arrange, to make ready, to prepare."

---

*In half a minute Mrs. Cratchit entered—flushed, but smiling proudly—with the pudding, like a speckled cannon-ball, so hard and firm, blazing in half of half-a-quartern of ignited brandy, and **bedight** with Christmas holly stuck into the top.*

— A CHRISTMAS CAROL

The Cratchit's Christmas pudding usually leaves modern (American) readers begging for an explanation. Ostensibly, it was a cross between a big boiled dumpling and a boozy fruitcake—quite the titillating combination for Victorian taste buds. But the pomp and pageantry of the pudding—which Dickens makes so memorable—was by far its most delicious claim to fame. Its preparations began in late November, when the pudding's ingredients were combined and mixed on the quasi-holiday known as Stir-up Sunday. Traditionally, everyone in the family would have a go at stirring the mixture (as doing so was said to bring enormous luck). Then it was tied up in a cloth and boiled for hours before hibernating in a cool larder until December 25th (a sufficient quantity of brandy in the pudding prevented it from spoiling). On Christmas Day another long boil reheated the pudding in preparation for the pièce de résistance: when the pudding was turned out on a platter, topped with a sprig of holly, ignited with more brandy, and marched proudly into the dining room, fabulously engulfed in blue flames—the crowning glory of the Victorian Christmas dinner.

Calculating Boy

[KAL-kyuh-lay-ting·boi] A mathematical prodigy.

In the parlour of one of these [crowded] houses . . . hung a bill, announcing that there was yet one room to let within its walls, though on what story the vacant room could be . . . it would have been beyond the power of a **calculating boy** *to discover.*

— NICHOLAS NICKLEBY

Dickens is obviously thinking of George Bidder, the era's real-life calculating boy, or "calculating phenomenon" as he was known to his contemporaries. At age seven, Bidder, the son of a stonemason, astonished his local village with his uncanny math skills (he couldn't even read yet). So naturally, Bidder's father made the most of it, turning his son into an academic sideshow and touring "the calculating phenomenon" throughout Britain. And by all accounts, Bidder's computing brain was truly phenomenal. He could answer any ponderously large arithmetical problem at lightning speed. Even Queen Charlotte got to test his abilities. One of her questions: what number multiplied by itself will produce 36,372,961? Bidder answered "6,031" in eight seconds flat. Obviously impressed by Bidder, Dickens used the term "calculating boy" again in *Hard Times*, though he seemed to find the whole human-calculator thing somewhat unsettling. In the novel, the character of Bitzer (sound familiar?) is another child genius, though he turns out to be nothing but a cold, calculating villain as an adult.

Caul

[kawl] A portion of the amniotic sac that, on rare occasions, remains intact and surrounds an infant's head at birth, from the French *cale*, a type of cap.

---

*I was born with a **caul**, which was advertised for sale, in the newspapers, at the low price of fifteen guineas.*

— DAVID COPPERFIELD

Today, a whole book could be written on David Copperfield's *caul*—certainly one of the oddest anatomical objects in English literature and one bursting with complex, symbolic potential. But for Victorian readers, it would have been a bit more straightforward. In an age when every normal birth was truly miraculous, due to the era's high infant mortality, a child born with a dangerous sack of fluid enveloping his or her head was phenomenally rare; and to have survived the ordeal would imbue the child with almost mythical qualities. This means that David's "I was born with a caul" brag effectively translates to: *I was born to be special* (though we could have gathered that from the novel's title). The really special thing about caul babies, though, was their supposed immunity against drowning—another consequence of their coming into the world with a watery helmet on. By association, the caul itself was viewed as a powerful talisman against drowning, which is why David's gets sold to the highest superstitious bidder. In hindsight, he should have held more tightly to his caul. Steerforth could have sure used it in Chapter 55.

Celestial Nine

[suh-LES-chuhl·nahyn] The classical Greek muses, nine in total, said to be the divine imparters of artistic creativity.

---

*Miss Twinkleton resumed her writing . . . biting the end of her pen, and looking upward, as waiting for the descent of an idea from any member of the **Celestial Nine** who might have one to spare.*

— THE MYSTERY OF EDWIN DROOD

To his reading public, it seemed as if Dickens never experienced Miss Twinkleton's dilemma. Rather, it looked like he had the Celestial Nine on speed dial: inventing, conceptualizing, and writing new stories faster than any of his contemporaries. "Invention," Dickens even admitted, "seems the easiest thing in the world," with literary ideas usually coming so fast and frequently into his head that he'd often complain of not having enough publishing space in which to fit them all. These were Dickens' good days, the products of which always caused people to naturally assume that writing was effortless for him—an assumption that made Dickens chuckle. He certainly had his bad days. And those, as he describes in a late-night letter to a friend, made Miss Twinkleton's dilemma look positively delightful:

Your note finds me settling myself to Little Dorrit again, and in the usual wretchedness of such settlement—which is unsettlement. Prowling about the rooms, sitting down, getting up, stirring the fire, looking out of window, tearing my hair, sitting down to write, writing nothing, writing something and tearing it up, going out, coming in, a Monster to my family, a dread Phenomenon to myself."

Choleric

[KOL-er-ik] Irritable, hot-tempered, literally suffering from too much bodily *choler*, "yellow bile"—one of the four classical humors (see below).

> *He did no work for two or three years before he died, but lived in clover; and his last act (like a **choleric** old gentleman) was to kick his doctor.*

> **— THE OLD CURIOSITY SHOP**

Associated nowadays with medieval medicine, humoral theory essentially promoted the idea that human bodies were composed of four elemental fluids or *humors* (from the Latin for "moisture"). These were blood, phlegm, yellow bile, and black bile. "Good humored" individuals were said to have their fluids in proper balance, enjoying good health and an even-keeled personality. Everyone else was, in some way, humorally challenged. Those with an excess of blood were considered *sanguine* (from Latin for "blood"), by far the best imbalance to have as it was thought to make you more cheery and optimistic. What, after all, would Mr. Micawber do without his "sanguine temper"? Too much phlegm, by contrast, was believed to make you quiet and reserved. Note the "phlegmatic temperament" of Mr. Barkis in *David Copperfield*, the excessively calm cart driver with the tersest marriage proposal in English literature: "Barkis is willin.'" There was nothing worse, however, than an excess of black bile (what the French called *meloncolie*), which always led to depression and low spirits, with no greater sufferer of this than Mr. Venus, the miserable "melancholy man" in *Our Mutual Friend*.

Climacteric

[kly-MAK-ter-ik] In ancient Greek numerology, *climacterics* were critical stages, or turning points, in a person's life, occurring every seven years. One's sixty-third year was considered especially significant, the "grand climacteric," as it were.

---

*In the ball-room . . . were divers unmarried ladies past their grand **climacteric**, who, not dancing because there were no partners for them, and not playing cards lest they should be set down as irretrievably single, were in the favourable situation of being able to abuse everybody without reflecting on themselves.*

— THE PICKWICK PAPERS

Why are these old ladies so haughty? It's probably because they have a sneaking suspicion that they're going to outlive all the young rascals in the ballroom. And for good reason. According to popular Victorian thought, if a woman (or man) could reach the grand-climacteric year of sixty-three in relatively good health, she was seen as being virtually inoculated against the diseases of midlife and was well on her way to an extremely ripe old age. "So general is this belief," read a mid-nineteenth-century medical dictionary,* "that the passing of sixty generally gives much anxiety to most people." Though once over this grand-climacteric hill, the triumphant lady could be assured, continued the dictionary, of easily expecting her life span to "be protracted to ninety"—an extraordinary claim that must have disappointed countless readers.

*Lexicon Medicum: Or, Medical Dictionary by Robert Hooper, 1845

Conchological

[kong-ko-LOJ-i-kuhl] Relating to the study of shells, especially mollusk shells, from the Greek *konkhe*, "a shell."

---

*The little Gradgrinds had cabinets in various departments of science too. They had a little **conchological** cabinet, and a little metallurgical cabinet, and a little mineralogical cabinet.*

— HARD TIMES

If you had a conchological collection in Victorian England, August 5th was your day to cash in. Known as Oyster Day, the traditional start of the oyster season, it conveniently coincided with the feast day of Saint James (whose symbolic emblem was a shell). It was, therefore, in theoretical honor of Saint James that children gathered on August 5th to build little heaps of oyster shells in jack-o'-lantern fashion: constructing their "grottos" on street corners and placing a lighted candle inside. Then, with an empty shell in hand, they began accosting passersby with the irresistible beg: "Please to remember the grotto—only once a year." Their profits were meant to be later distributed to the needy—though anyone who believed *that* was just hallucinating after a bad oyster.

Contumaciously

[kon-too-MAY-shuhs-lee] In a stubborn or willfully disobedient manner, from the Latin *contumax*, "insolent, obstinate."

"Trouble¿" echoed my sister, "trouble¿" And then entered on a fearful catalogue of all the illnesses I [Pip] had been guilty of . . . and all the times she had wished me in my grave, and I had **contumaciously** *refused to go there.*

— GREAT EXPECTATIONS

Pip's contumacious refusal to die must have been incredibly strong. Aside from his sister's murderous wishes, Pip's greatest threat to life is that he is simply born a Victorian. And all Victorian children lived precariously close to the grave. In this prevaccine world, child mortality rates were consistently high; throughout the century roughly one out of seven children died before the age of one. In some urban areas, one-half of all deaths involved children under the age five. Numbers like these skewed the era's life expectancy (averaging around forty years). It wasn't actually that miraculous, or rare, for Victorians to move through their middle years into old age. The miracle was getting through childhood alive. Faced with these odds, Dickens was considered a very lucky parent. He fathered six children who lived beyond their forties, with many living well beyond that (his daughter Katey almost made it to ninety). Two of his sons did die in their twenties, but only one daughter, named Dora, died in infancy. *Only* is a relative term, of course, and most Victorians never got used to living with these deathly statistics.

Dropsical

[DROP-si-kuhl] Bloated, swollen, often in a humorous way, *dropsy* being the old term for edema (bodily swelling caused by an excess of watery fluids).

---

*The Six Jolly Fellowship-Porters, already mentioned as a tavern of a **dropsical** appearance, had . . . a narrow lopsided wooden jumble of corpulent windows heaped one upon another as you might heap as many toppling oranges.*

— OUR MUTUAL FRIEND

It's so typically Dickensian that the snuggest, coziest tavern in his fiction would be described as "dropsical." Dickens always had a literary infatuation with bloatedness, corpulence, and pleasantly-plumpness, which usually indicated benevolence in his allegorical mind. From the very beginning, an almost perfectly-round Mr. Pickwick "burst like another sun" onto the page, his solar rotundity an obvious reflector of his large-hearted generosity. Then there's the affectionate Clara Peggoty in *David Copperfield* who, "being very plump," would lose "some of the buttons on the back of her gown" every time she squeezes David in a hug. Even the exacerbating Mr. Turveydrop, the "fat old gentleman . . . pinched in, and swelled out" in *Bleak House* is absolutely harmless (note his dropsical name, the *drop* in Turveydrop isn't a coincidence), thanks very much to the benignity of bigness that Dickens can't help but embrace.

Flitch of Bacon

[flich·uhv·BAY-kuhn] The proverbial prize for matrimonial bliss, a *flitch* ("side") of bacon was historically awarded to the most loving and unquarrelsome couple in the English village of Dunmow.

> *And dear Mrs. Lammle and dear Mr. Lammle [said Lady Tippins], how do you do, and when are you going down to what's-its-name place . . . what is it?—Dun Cow—to claim the* **flitch of bacon***?*

— OUR MUTUAL FRIEND

Here's something that even Dickens' imagination could never have dreamt up: the famous "Dunmow Flitch Trials"—ancient England's own not-so-newlywed game. Every four years (since the twelfth century, some say), the village of Dunmow in the Essex countryside has offered up a flitch of bacon to any couple who could prove they had not argued for one whole year and a day. A village court was established to test the applicants' claims (Dunmow doesn't give out its pork easily), and the couple who could endure the trial got to bring home the literal bacon. The first blissful couple, the legend goes, earned their flitch in 1104. That date may be a bit early, though Chaucer casually alludes to the "bacon . . . at Dunmow" in *The Canterbury Tales* (as if everyone already knew what it was by the fourteenth century). His Wife of Bath makes the rather obvious point that none of her horrible husbands were fit for the prize at Dunmow. And neither, of course, are Mr. and Mrs. Lammle, no matter how much Lady Tippins rubs it in.

Foot-pace

[foot-pays] Walking speed.

> *Mr. Carker the Manager rode on at a **foot-pace**, with the easy air of one who had performed all the business of the day in a satisfactory manner, and got it comfortably off his mind.*
>
> — DOMBEY AND SON

"If I could not walk far and fast," Dickens told a friend, "I think I should just explode and perish." Enjoy the moment, because this is one of the rare occasions when Dickens isn't exaggerating. Walking was truly crucial to his psyche, helping to abate his chronic feelings of "restlessness" and constant cravings for inspiration beyond his writing desk. Consequently, Dickens devoured roads at far more than a foot-pace. A strenuous "four miles an hour" was his usual walking speed, earning him the nickname "the Elastic Novice" from his friends. But even if his friends could have kept up, Dickens wasn't the best of walking companions, as he had a tendency to slip into perambulating trances. On one early-morning walk through the Kentish countryside, Dickens purportedly "fell asleep to the monotonous sound of my own feet." By breakfast, he had ended up in London, a whopping thirty miles away. And all this "without the slightest sense of exertion." We told you Dickens liked to exaggerate.

Graminivorous

[gram-uh-NIV-er-uhs] A Latin loanword meaning "feeding on grass."

> *I made a perfect victim of myself. I even entertained some idea*
> *of putting myself on a vegetable diet, vaguely conceiving that, in*
> *becoming a **graminivorous** animal, I should sacrifice to Dora.*
>
> — DAVID COPPERFIELD

While David Copperfield might be contemplating a graminivorous diet, the nineteenth-century vegetarian movement found no supporter in Charles Dickens. He had nothing against vegetables themselves (this, after all, was the man whose imagination was once fired by the smell of "faded cabbage leaves"), but he did hate any prohibitionist movement which, he believed, lacked perspective on the virtues of moderation. Like Victorian teetotalers and pacifists, he viewed "distinguished vegetarians" as quasi-religious extremists who preached an all-or-nothing, "whole hog" approach to their principles. Their sermons sounded something like this to Dickens' satirical ear:

> *It had been discovered that mankind at large can only be regenerated . . . by always dining on Vegetables . . . Stew so much as the bone of a mutton chop in the pot with your vegetables, and you will never make another Eden out of a Kitchen Garden. You must take the Whole Hog, Sir, and every bristle on him, or you and the rest of mankind will never be regenerated.*

Habiliments

[huh-BIL-eh-ments] Clothing, from the French *habiller*, "to dress."

> *The manager at once repaired to a small dressing-room, adjacent, where Mrs. Crummles was then occupied in exchanging the* **habiliments** *of a melodramatic empress for the ordinary attire of matrons in the nineteenth century.*
>
> — NICHOLAS NICKLEBY

That stout Mrs. Crummles has to squeeze into a small dressing room is just one of the disadvantages of her theatrical life—though it's a life that Dickens, on so many occasions, positively envied. In fact, in his younger years, he had his heart set on entering the acting profession: gobbling up every new stage play, taking acting lessons, and landing an audition with a famous London theater at the age of twenty. Though, as fate would fantastically have it, on the day of the audition Dickens came down with a bad head cold, missed the tryout, and decided, from them on, to give his other love, writing, a second chance. God bless head colds! But Dickens never entirely gave up on the actor within. He did have to settle for performing in amateur theatricals put on by his friends and family, but even those filled him with an excitement that could only be matched by the thrill of writing. Putting on plays, he said, was "like writing a book in company. A satisfaction of a most singular kind, which has no exact parallel in my life."

Homeopathic Doses

[hoh-mee-uh-PATH-ik·DOHS-iz] Infinitesimally small amounts.

---

*Mounting a stool, [Fagin] cautiously applied his eye to the pane of glass, from which secret post he could see Mr. Claypole taking cold beef from the dish, and porter from the pot, and administering **homeopathic doses** of both to Charlotte.*

— OLIVER TWIST

Homeopathy was one of the many miracle cures of the Victorian age—or so it hoped to be. Introduced by the physician Samuel Hahnemann in 1810, homeopathy's most popular principal was the "Law of Infinitesimals." Basically, it asserted that medicine was only effective in incredibly small quantities—a real less is more belief that Dickens parodies in the phrase "homeopathic doses." And while Dickens briefly tried homeopathy (as an unsuccessful cure of his chronic colds), he obviously preferred making fun of it. In *The Mudfog Papers*, Mr. Pipkin relates the story of a certain Sir William Courtenay, a staunch believer in the Law of Infinitesimals. Sir William is such a believer that he hires a peasant woman to follow him around, administering homeopathic doses of medicine whenever he finds himself close to death. But when Sir William gets shot, the woman hasn't a clue what to do. Mr. Pipkin concludes that "an infinitesimal dose of lead and gunpowder" would have done the trick. But alas, "the woman concerned did not possess the power of reasoning" by homeopathy and Sir William dies, having "been sacrificed to the ignorance of the peasantry."

Ligneous

[LIG-nee-uhs] Made of, or resembling, wood, from Latin *lignum*, "wood."

---

*Much impressed by . . . the friendly disposition of Mr. Wegg, as exemplified in his so soon dropping into poetry, Mr. Boffin again shook hands with that **ligneous** sharper.*

— OUR MUTUAL FRIEND

Mr. Wegg is a "ligneous sharper" for good reason: a *sharper* (see page 127) for his blackmailing propensities and *ligneous* for his wooden leg—one of the most famous wooden legs in English literature, though certainly not Dickens' first. Thirteen of his novels make reference to some sort of ligneous appendage, from Sam's wooden-leg joke in *The Pickwick Papers* to the frightening teacher Mr. Tungay, "the man with the wooden leg," in *David Copperfield*. Literary critics have made a stupendous bonfire out of all the wooden-leggedness in Dickens' writing, interpreting the limbs as symbolic embodiments (or disembodiments) of Dickensian themes of comedy, pathos, and horror. The simpler explanation is that Dickens was, as always, simply writing what he observed: that the Victorian world was surprisingly full of real wooden-legged characters. Wooden legs were mainstream prosthetics in the nineteenth century—a world where the amputation of limbs was alarmingly mundane. They were so common that, according to Mr. Vuffin in *The Old Curiosity Shop*, "if you was to advertise [a play performed] entirely by wooden legs, it's my belief you wouldn't draw a sixpence."

Lucubration

[loo-kyoo-BRAY-shuhn] An elaborate, often overelaborate, piece of writing, from the Latin *lucubrare*, "to work by candlelight," as presumably most overelaborate writing is composed in the dead of night.

---

*Wolf . . . recited the leading points of one or two vastly humorous articles he was then preparing. These **lucubrations** being of what he called "a warm complexion," were highly approved; and all the company agreed that they were full of point.*

— MARTIN CHUZZLEWIT

Not everyone approved of Dickens' lucubrations. And lucubrations he certainly had. Ten out of his fifteen novels run to eight hundred or more pages long, giving rise to the false, yet understandable, myth that Dickens was paid by the word. "The outstanding, unmistakable mark of Dickens's writing is the *unnecessary detail*," remarked George Orwell, the early twentieth-century writer. This sounds more like a backhanded compliment, as the delight of reading Dickens is precisely in those trivial details—a paradox that countless editors and critics have had to grapple with. In 1933, when Robert Graves embarked on an ambitious abridgement of *David Copperfield*, stripping its text of superfluous detail (and cutting out half of the book in the process), he unwittingly cut out all of its literary magic as well. Perhaps he should have paid more attention to David Copperfield's own thoughts on the matter: "We talk about the tyranny of words, but we like to tyrannize over them too; we are fond of having a large superfluous establishment of words to wait upon us."

Magnetic Slumber

[mag-NEH-tik·SLUHM-ber] A hypnotic trance, based on the pseudoscientific belief that a mystical magnetic force connected all living beings and that one person could control (or hypnotize) the magnetic force of another.

---

*Mr. and Mrs. Squeers drew close up to the fire, and sitting with their feet on the fender, talked confidentially in whispers; while Nicholas . . . [read a book] with as much thought or consciousness of what he was doing as if he had been in a **magnetic slumber**.*

— NICHOLAS NICKLEBY

The idea of a malleable magnetism between humans was popularized by the eighteenth-century Viennese physician Franz Anton Mesmer. Although laughed out of Austria for attempting to cure his patients with a rough form of hypnotism (then called "mesmerism," and from which our word *mesmerize* originates), Mesmer's ideas were enthusiastically embraced in England. The chance to be put into a magnetic slumber meant the chance to have your magnetic equilibrium put aright, and every imaginable ill cured. The difficulty in this method lay in finding an "operator," literally a more strongly magnetized person, to perform the therapy. It's hardly surprising, given his magnetic personality, but Dickens (from the 1830s onwards) became convinced that he had enormous "operator" potential and went about mesmerizing his friends and relatives whenever he could. In 1844 he performed a months' long mesmerizing therapy on a woman he met in Italy, sometimes treating her in her bedroom, and incurring the very understandable ire of Catherine (his wife) in the process.

Mephistophelean

[mef-i-stuh-FEE-lee-uhn] Devilishly cunning, after the devil in the German legend of Faust, known for his diabolical delight in trickery.

---

*The room door opening at this crisis of Miss Tox's feelings, she started, laughed aloud, and fell into the arms of the person entering; happily insensible . . . of the Major at his window over the way . . . whose face and figure were dilated with **Mephistophelean** joy.*

— DOMBEY AND SON

The devil lurks everywhere in Dickens' fiction, mostly popping up in the word "deuce"—as in Dickens' often-used phrase, "What the deuce!" A mild Victorian oath, it relied on *deuce* serving as a gentle euphemism for the devil (because swearing by the devil outright was too strong for Victorian sensibilities). How *deuce* acquired its devilish reputation is open to colorful speculation, though it could be as simple as the fact that a *deuce* is a two in a deck of cards or a pair of dice, and the devil has two horns. Of course, the devil has many nicknames, and one in particular continues to haunt Dickens' legacy, as it does with this very book. "What the dickens!" is synonymous with "What the deuce!" with *dickens* serving as another old English euphemism for the devil, predating Charles Dickens by some three hundred years. Though lost on us today, Charles was well aware of this association, as was his reading public. One anonymous Victorian reviewer pointed out: "Mr. Dickens, as if in revenge for his own queer name, does bestow still queerer ones upon his fictitious creations."

Monomania

[mon-oh-MAY-nee-uh] A popular nineteenth-century catchword for an excessive preoccupation with one thing, from the Greek *mono*, "one," and *mania*, "mad passion."

---

*No, really, my dear Doctor, you must excuse me if I appear to dwell on this rather, because I feel so very strongly. I call it quite my **monomania**, it is such a subject of mine.*

— DAVID COPPERFIELD

By and large, Dickensian characters are all hopeless monomaniacs (linguistically speaking). Most are obsessively preoccupied with one catchy expression: Scrooge has his "humbugs!" and Mr. Micawber his perennial conviction that "something will turn up." These catchphrases, technically known as *tags*, are a signature part of Dickens' style. And the majority of readers, then and now, have found the simple predictability of these expressions a delightful component of the Dickensian experience, quickly connecting them to the comic hearts of his characters. Readers less charmed by repetition should stay clear of *David Copperfield*, the most tag-full novel in Dickens' collection. Among its tag-loving characters: Uriah Heep is ever "so 'umble," Mrs. Gummidge is "a lone lorn creetur'," Mrs. Micawber always insists that "I never will desert Mr. Micawber," and Betsey Trotwood interrupts almost every serious conversation with "Janet! Donkeys!"

Mumchance

[MUHM-chans] Silent.

> *"Father," returned Joe . . . "Look at other young men of my age. Have they no liberty, no will, no right to speak? Are they obliged to sit **mumchance**, and to be ordered about till they are the laughing-stock of young and old?"*
>
> — BARNABY RUDGE

Perhaps this is a good time to remind Joe that mumchance used to be rather fun. Mumchance, in fact, was the name of a gambling dice game in the sixteenth century. It had one important rule: that the players kept *mum*,* or quiet, throughout the game—hence the word's later link with silence. The other rules of mumchance are, unfortunately, lost to the gaming tables of history, but many historians assume that it was similar to *hazard*—a medieval precursor to the modern game of craps that was still played in Dickens' day. Though we can safely assume that Dickens would have hated mumchance, as he hated nearly all forms of gambling—a personal conviction he pounds over the head of every reader of *The Old Curiosity Shop*.

---

*Dating back to the fourteenth century, *mum* is a purely onomatopoeic word, meaning its origin lies in the sound it seeks to imitate—in this case, the sound of "mmm," the only real sound a person can make when his or her mouth is firmly closed.

N.B.

[en-bee] An abbreviation of the Latin phrase *nota bene*, "note well" or "take notice."

I opened the door to the company . . . and last of all to Uncle Pumblechook. **N.B.** *I was not allowed to call him uncle, under the severest penalties.*

— BLEAK HOUSE

When readers come across an abbreviated word or phrase in Dickens' works, they're actually looking at the tip of a massive intellectual iceberg that sinks deep into his past. Though few of his abbreviations have survived in published form, Dickens could write, and often did write, in shorthand with astonishing aptitude. "I dare say I am at this present [moment] the best shorthand writer in the world," Dickens wrote to a friend—a boast he could only make after years of arduous practice. Before he became a novelist, a sixteen-year-old Dickens forced himself to learn shorthand in application for a job as a parliamentary reporter. Then known as the "Gurney system," shorthand was a totally new and bizarre language of hieroglyphic-like symbols. Its learning curve was steep—so steep, it "was almost heartbreaking" for Dickens. And since his personal miseries always loved fictional company, years later Dickens couldn't resist giving David Copperfield the same challenge. He, too, must learn the Gurney system, famously beating his head over that "savage stenographic mystery."

Noisome

[NOI-suhm] Repulsively offensive, especially in regards to smell; a formal Victorian adjective based on the Middle English word *noy*, an obsolete relative to our modern verb "annoy."

---

*Extraordinary how soon the **noisome** flavour of imprisoned sleep, becomes manifest in all such places that are ill-cared for!*

— A TALE OF TWO CITIES

The most noisome event in Dickens' day was, without question, the fantastically named "Great Stink" of 1858. London's river Thames was the culprit, as it was the chief dumping ground for most of the city's waste, human and otherwise, at the time. "Through the heart of the town a deadly sewer ebbed and flowed, in the place of a fine fresh river," wrote Dickens in *Little Dorrit,* shortly before the polluted river finally protested its historic abuse. It only took the unusually hot, dry summer of 1858 for that to happen. The river's waste literally began cooking in the scorching sun, sending up a putrid stench that Dickens described as "head-and-stomach distracting." Parliament hastily agreed (housed uncomfortably close to the river itself) and within a month, an "Act for the Purification of the Thames" was passed, legislating the start of London's first modern sewer system.

Nonage

[NON-ij] The period of childhood or immaturity, from a Middle English compound literally meaning "not of age."

---

*There was the dreary Sunday of his childhood. . . . There was the sleepy Sunday of his boyhood. . . . There was the interminable Sunday of his **nonage**.*

— LITTLE DORRIT

Arthur Clennam's dreary childhood in *Little Dorrit* underscores the darker side of Victorian child rearing. Influenced by the nineteenth-century revival of Puritanism, it held firm to the belief in children's inborn wickedness and the importance of stamping out all manifestations of original sin. Dickens vehemently disagreed with this "gloomy theology," satirizing it in *David Copperfield* as an irrational doctrine that "made all children out to be a swarm of little vipers." Though, ever the moderate, Dickens was careful not to swing in the opposite direction and embrace the equally extreme idea (popularized by the Romantic poets) that all children were totally innocent and wholly angelic. Refuting such a "lamentable" sentiment in *Our Mutual Friend*, Dickens portrays Charley Hexam's disorderly school as suffering from a serious case of scholastic denial: "the place was pervaded by a grimly ludicrous pretense that every pupil was childish and innocent."

Orthography

[or-THOG-ruh-fee] Correct and conventional spelling, from the Greek for "correct writing."

---

*In the course of the night, also, the following phenomena had occurred. Bishop Butler had insisted on spelling his name, "Bubler," for which offence against **orthography** and good manners he had been dismissed as out of temper.*

— THE HAUNTED HOUSE

For the man who said, "nobody can write properly without spelling well," Dickens certainly had a way of circumventing his own advice. As all readers have discovered (either to their charm or consternation), Dickens was a prolific user of *eye dialect*—spelling words as they are pronounced, not as they are actually spelled. And since most speakers in Victorian society didn't bother with proper grammar and articulation, Dickens recorded, in a real sense, only what he heard. And every Dickensian fan rejoices at that fact: the fact that Dickens used his ear (and not his dictionary) when writing dialogue, the fact that readers are almost forced to mouth the conversations of his more incomprehensible characters, a literary trick that Dickens knew would infuse them with unparalleled realism. Though this realism obviously gave Anthony Trollope a massive headache: "Of Dickens's style it is impossible to speak in praise. It is jerky, ungrammatical, and created by himself in defiance of rules." It certainly is.

Perspicuously

[per-SPIK-yoo-uhs-lee] In a clear, easily understood manner, from Latin *perspicuous*, "transparent."

> *I had been reading to Peggotty about crocodiles. I must have read very **perspicuously**, or the poor soul must have been deeply interested, for I remember she had a cloudy impression, after I had done, that they were a sort of vegetable.*
>
> — DAVID COPPERFIELD

Perspicuity was of prime importance to Dickens. It was literally his bread-and-butter, as his voice was once just as popular as his pen, and he relied heavily on public readings of his stories to supplement his income. Thankfully, Dickens enjoyed a clear, well-defined voice in a "rather loose mouth," according to his friend Thomas Carlyle. And Dickens apparently believed his loose mouth was a biological gift, one to be inherited by all ten of his children. Nothing else could account for the shock he experienced as a result of his eight-year-old son Frank. "I find," he wrote one morning to a friend, "to my great vexation and distress . . . that Frank stammers so horribly as to be quite an afflicted object." How Frank's stammer went undetected by Dickens for so many years is a moot point, though one he personally didn't dwell on. Instead, Dickens set about immediately loosening Frank's mouth himself, calling his son into his office every morning and having him recite long passages from Shakespeare until, according to his other son Alfred, "my Father made a complete cure of him."

Phantasmagoria

[fan-taz-muh-GOHR-ee-uh] A primitive Victorian slide projector that could make images (usually frightening images) grow and shrink from view.

---

*Quilp said not a word in reply, but walking so close to Kit as to bring his eyes within two or three inches of his face, looked fixedly at him, retreated a little distance without averting his gaze, approached again, again withdrew, and so on for half-a-dozen times, like a head in a **phantasmagoria**.*

— THE OLD CURIOSITY SHOP

From the Greek noun *phantasma* ("ghost, specter"), the phantasmagoria show was the closest thing Victorians could get to watching a horror flick. First performed in the 1790s, the spectacle remained much the same into Dickens' day. Sitting in a dark room in front of a transparent screen, the audience would be spooked stiff by an array of ghoulish images that seemed to shrink and grow before their very eyes, often to uncomfortably close proportions. Behind the screen and hidden from view, a (no doubt very amused) young man was busily engaged in exciting every horrified scream by simply rolling a movable projector closer to and farther from the screen.

Plumbless

[PLUHM-les] Immeasurably deep, based on the fact that old depth measuring devices had lead weights attached to their ends (*plume* being the Latin word for "lead").

---

*The moment shot away into the **plumbless** depths of the past, to mingle with all the lost opportunities that are drowned there.*

— HARD TIMES

Since *plumbing* also shares a root with the Latin word for lead (this time in reference to lead pipes), most Victorians could accurately be considered very plumb-*less* indeed. By midcentury, indoor plumbing and flushable toilets were only enjoyed by the wealthiest households, leaving the rest with one unpleasant alternative. Deep pits were dug in back gardens, as far away from the house as possible, over which a simple structure containing a makeshift toilet was suspended. One of the foulest facts of Victorian life, these "cesspits," sometimes shared by multiple families, tended to fill up embarrassingly fast. At such awkward times, their heaping contents would have to be emptied and hauled away by "night-soil men"—an occupational word that, thankfully, has fallen out of existence, as *night soil* was the polite Victorian term for "human excrement."

Post-prandial

[pohst-PRAN-dee-uhl] Occurring after a meal (usually meaning after dinner), from the Latin *post*, "after," and *prandium*, "a meal."

---

*The good-natured Reverdy Johnson, being at an Art Dinner in Glasgow the other night, and falling asleep over the **post-prandial** speeches (only too naturally) woke suddenly on hearing the name of 'Johnson' in a list of Scotch painters . . . [and] at once plunged up, under the impression that somebody was drinking his health, and immediately, and with overflowing amiability began returning thanks.*

— LETTERS OF CHARLES DICKENS

Having an enviable mix of introverted and extroverted tendencies, Dickens was as charming a speechmaker as he was a writer. "He spoke so well," wrote Anthony Trollope, "that a public dinner became a blessing instead of a curse, if he was in the chair." And Dickens was in the "chair" a lot. He spoke at an endless round of society dinners, charity functions, and publicity stints—anywhere his celebrity was demanded. But remarkably he didn't find the need to write any of his speeches down, preferring instead to keep all the particular points in his "mind's eye." When asked how he managed to extemporize so eloquently, Dickens told his manager that he pictorially likened the speech "to the tire of a cart wheel—he being the hub. From the hub to the tire he would run as many spokes as there were subjects to be treated [in the speech]; and during the progress of the speech he would deal with each spoke separately, elaborating them as he went round the wheel."

Pot-valiant

[pot-VAL-yuhnt] Made courageous and bold through drunkenness. *Pot* was a generic term for a drinking vessel, usually one that held alcohol, from the Latin *potus*, "drinking cup."

"Perhaps we had better retire," whispered Mr. Pickwick. "Never, sir," rejoined Pott, **pot-valiant** *in a double sense, "never."*

— THE PICKWICK PAPERS

By all accounts a restrained and moderate drinker, there were times when Dickens greatly relied on the pot-valiant effects of alcohol. In 1868, fatigued by failing health, Dickens punctuated his arduous publicity tour of America with a clockwork "system" of stimulating drinks. Writing to his daughter in England, he describes his almost entirely alcoholic diet:

At seven in the morning, in bed, a tumbler of new cream and two tablespoons of rum. At twelve, a sherry cobbler [sherry, sugar, lemon and ice] and a biscuit. At three (dinner time), a pint of champagne. At five minutes to eight, an egg beaten up with a glass of sherry . . . and anything to drink that I can fancy. I don't eat more than half a pound of solid food in the whole four-and-twenty hours, if so much.

Pusillanimous

[pyoo-si-LAN-ih-muhs] Contemptibly timid in mind and spirit, literally "small-souled," from the Latin *pusillus*, "little," and *animus*, "spirit or soul."

> *"You lie!" said the Manager, red with sudden anger . . . "You **pusillanimous**, abject, cringing dogs! All making the same show, all canting the same story, all whining the same professions, all harbouring the same transparent secret."*
>
> — DOMBEY AND SON

Pronounced correctly (with all its s's emphasized), *pusillanimous* offers the rare treat to hiss at your enemies, without losing your sophistication or pride. A serpentine word if ever there was one; it's no coincidence that Dickens bequeathed this obscure English adjective to the character of James Carker, office manager of Dombey and Son. The archvillain of the book, Carker is often described in snakelike language* with a hideous mouth that can stretch like an anaconda, "as if it were made of India-rubber."

*Though when it comes to snaky characters, no one can out-slither Uriah Heep in *David Copperfield*. Dickens doesn't beat around the metaphorical bush with him. Heep is "that detestable serpent," "clammy" to the touch, always twisting and writhing "in his slimy way," a "crawling impersonation of meanness."

Quondam

[KWON-duhm] Former, that once was, from the Latin for "formerly."

> *Mrs. Weller . . . the rather stout lady was no other than the* **quondam** *relict and sole executrix of the dead-and-gone Mr. Clarke.*
>
> — THE PICKWICK PAPERS

That Dickens is now popularly associated with the fantasy of "Merry Olde England" would have surely made his progressive blood boil. In life, he always tried to distance himself from the quondam relics of the past. A thoroughly modern and forward-looking man, Dickens was "thankful for the privilege of living in this summer-dawn of time" and mostly had a negative view of previous ages in England's history. Those were the ages "of darkness, wickedness, and violence," says the Goblin in *The Chimes*. And Dickens lambasted anyone who yearned for the supposed "good old times." *What good old times?* Dickens asks, "The good old times for cutting throats that cried out in their need?" As if to remind himself not to commit a similar folly, he had a series of caustically clever dummy books made for his personal library. Titled, in full, *The Wisdom of our Ancestors*, it contained the lesser volumes of *Ignorance*, *Superstition*, *The Block*, *The Stake*, *The Rack*, *Dirt*, and *Disease*.

Self-snatchation

[self-snatch-AY-shuhn] To snatch yourself from something, especially from something dangerous.

---

*I am precipitated into the abyss, and have no power of **self-snatchation** (forgive me if I coin that phrase) from the yawning gulf before me.*

— MASTER HUMPHREY'S CLOCK

Unlike this poor soul, the innate power of self-snatchation proved pivotal in Dickens' life and subsequent rise to fame. From sheer dogged determination he was able to snatch himself from childhood poverty (working in a boot polish factory) to become one of the wealthiest and most well-known writers in history. How did he do it? The phrase "self-denial" repeatedly comes up in his letters—a clue to his laborious devotion to writing, for which he sometimes turned out four thousand words a day and often worked into the early-morning hours to meet an endless barrage of deadlines. Naturally Dickens has his most autobiographical character, David Copperfield, elaborate on "the source of my success": "I never could have done what I have done, without the habits of punctuality, order, and diligence, without the determination to concentrate myself on one subject at a time, no matter how quickly its successor should come upon its heels."

Seriatim

[seer-ee-AY-tim] Latin for "one after another."

> *After a vast deal of shaking of hands, and many remarks how they had never spent such a delightful evening . . . Mr. and Mrs. Kenwigs replied, by thanking every lady and gentleman, **seriatim**, for the favour of their company, and hoping they might have enjoyed themselves only half as well as they said they had.*
>
> — NICHOLAS NICKLEBY

Mostly used in legal jargon, *seriatim* is one of the words Dickens probably overheard in his teens while apprenticed to the law firm of Ellis and Blackmore—a position he held for well over a year. Always a keen observer, Dickens could soon imitate the vernacular of every clerk in the office. But thankfully, for the comprehension of his lower-class readership, Dickens never took his acquired legalese too seriously,* as Sam Weller reminds us in *The Pickwick Papers*: "Here's a subpoena for you, Mr. Weller," said Jackson. "What's that in English?" inquired Sam.

---

*Dickens' knowledge of Latin was actually quite slim by Victorian standards. That he knew "little Latin and less Greek" was one of the snobby criticisms of fellow writer William Makepeace Thackeray. But then again, Thackeray was always trying to outsmart and outwrite Dickens—a competition that Dickens seemed totally oblivious to (probably because he was always winning it).

Simoom

[si-MOOM] A hot, sandy wind—the sort of dry, suffocating wind that blows across Arabian deserts, from the Arabic *samum*, "poisonous."

> Clennam tried to do honour to the meal, but unavailingly . . . the bread seemed to turn to sand in his mouth . . . and the ham (though it was good enough of itself) seemed to blow a faint **simoom** of ham through the whole Marshalsea [prison].
>
> — LITTLE DORRIT

Victorian England was no Arabian desert, but its industrial cities had their own simooms of sorts. With every chimney puffing out soot and with poorly paved roads sending up clouds of chalky dust, London became, as Dickens called it, a "suburban Sahara" in dry, windy weather. In *Our Mutual Friend*, the "grating wind" of London "sawed rather than blew . . . Every street was a sawpit . . . every passenger was an under-sawyer, with the sawdust blinding him and choking him." Efforts were made to curtail this problem: city streets were watered regularly to cut down on the dust, and "dustmen" periodically hauled off unwanted cinders and ashes from London's fireplaces. Actually, dustmen would haul away any household rubbish available, hoping to recycle it for a nice profit later on (note the mountainous "dust-heaps" in *Our Mutual Friend* that make the Boffins incredible rich). Interestingly, the word *dust* as a generic term for garbage still survives in Britain today, where trash cans remain better known as "dustbins."

Succedaneum

[suhk-si-DAY-nee-uhm] A   substitute,   from   the   Latin *succedanues*, "following after or replacing."

> *Immediately there appeared, coming slowly up above the bulk-head of the cabin, another bulk-head—human, and very large. . . . The head was followed by a perfect desert of chin, and by a shirt-collar and neckerchief, and by a dread-nought pilot-coat, and by a pair of dreadnought pilot-trousers, whereof the waistband was so very broad and high, that it became a **succedaneum** for a waistcoat.*
>
> — **DOMBEY AND SON**

Pardon our indelicate observation, but this sailor's waistband, "so very broad and high," sounds an awful lot like a corset. "So what of it?" he might flippantly remark. Fair enough, as a variety of corsets were marketed directly to men throughout the Victorian era, mainly to help prop up the slouched figure (slouching being a cardinal sin of Victorian deportment, regardless of gender). "Recommended by doctors for gentleman," one 1893 advertisement sums up the rationale of the corseted male quite nicely:

> *Besides showing off the figure and enabling the tailor to ensure an effective fit and distinguished appearance, this combined Belt Corset is a necessity to most men for the promotion of health and comfort, together with an upright soldierly bearing. It expands the chest. It supports the spine, and holds the figure erect.*

Terpsichorean

[turp-si-KOHR-ee-uhn] Of or relating to dancing, from Terpsichore, the Greek goddess of dance.

---

*"[Dancing] is such a dreadful thing! If I was wicked enough—and strong enough—to kill anybody, it should be my partner." This was such an entirely new view of the **Terpsichorean** art as socially practised, that Mrs. Lammle looked at her young friend in some astonishment.*

— OUR MUTUAL FRIEND

Dickens would hardly have shared in these anti-terpsichorean sentiments, as his daughter Mamie recorded in *My Father as I Recall Him*:

My father was certainly not what in the ordinary acceptation of the term would be called "a good dancer." I doubt whether he had ever received any instruction in "the noble art" other than that which my sister and I gave him . . . [but] he was so fond of dancing. . . . Graceful in motion, his dancing, such as it was, was natural to him. Dance-music was delightful to his cheery, genial spirit; the time and steps of a dance suited his tidy nature, if I may so speak. The action and the exercise seemed to be a part of his abundant vitality.

---

*Dickens' favorite dance was the Sir Roger de Coverley (see page 40).

Tintinnabulation

[**tin-ti-nab-yuh-LAY-shuhn**] The sound of metallic ringing, especially the ringing of bells—an onomatopoeic word construction based on the Latin *tinnire*, "to ring."

---

*All the young gentlemen . . . gave a low groan. It was drowned in the **tintinnabulation** of the gong, which sounding again with great fury, there was a general move towards the dining-room.*

— DOMBEY AND SON

The tintinnabulation of gongs must have drowned out many a conversation in large Victorian households. Rung by a servant, usually three times a day, their brass clanged punctually at luncheon, one hour before dinner, and then again when dinner was served. Sometimes, however, gongs were given an early-morning beating, like the one that abruptly wakes up Paul in *Dombey and Son* with its "dreadful note of preparation," summoning him to morning prayers "down in the hall."

Versification

[vur-suh-fi-KAY-shuhn] The act of writing poetry, from the Latin *versificare*, "to make verses."

> *I was alone in the world, and much given to record that circumstance in fragments of English* **versification***.*
>
> — DAVID COPPERFIELD

David Copperfield is not as alone as he thinks. Finding solace in a sorrowful poem was the birthright of all Victorians needing a good cry. This was the golden age of "sentimental" poetry—a socially acceptable outlet for the emotionally suppressed Victorian. Dickens was caught up in it too. He cried over Thomas Hood's "The Bridge of Sighs" and sometimes repeated, in darker moods, the lamentable line from Tennyson's "Mariana": "I am aweary, aweary, I would that I were dead." Of course, this didn't stop Dickens from parodying the cloying excesses of this poetic style, most comically in *The Pickwick Papers* with the recitation of Mrs. Leo Hunter's "touching" poem, "Ode to an Expiring Frog":

> *Can I unmoved see thee dying*
> *On a log,*
> *Expiring frog!*